MORE TALES OF THE OLD
RAILWAYMEN

MORE TALES OF THE OLD
RAILWAYMEN

TOM QUINN

AURUM PRESS

First published in Great Britain
2002 by Aurum Press Ltd
25 Bedford Avenue, London WC1B 3AT

A catalogue record for this book is available
from the British Library.

Illustrations by Philip Murphy

Photographs on p. 2/3, 7, 55, 95 and 106/7
by Mike Spencer, courtesy of Milepost 92½
Picture Library

Other photographs courtesy of Reg Holmes,
David Lubbock, Stan Smith, Dick Potts,
Fred Simpson and Tom Quinn

Railway posters on p. 43, 47, 75, 79, 83, 111,
115, 151 and 155 courtesy of National Rail
Museum/Science and Society Picture Library

ISBN 1 85410 862 X

1 3 5 7 9 10 8 6 4 2
2002 2004 2006 2005 2003

Edited and designed by Sue Viccars and Les Dominey
at Blackingstone Books Ltd, Exeter

Printed in China by C.T. Printing

ACKNOWLEDGEMENTS

*Thanks to all the railwaymen who agreed to
talk to me, and to Sue and Les of Blackingstone
Books, who put the whole book together. Thanks
are also due to the following for help with text,
captions and research: J. Smith, K. Warren,
S. J. G., Emma Westall of Suchard,
C. Thompson, N. Bird, D. Fisher, L. Davis,
B. Thompson, L. P., S. Storey, S. B., Barry
Mcloughlin, Dave Ellis, Swindon's Steam
Museum, and C. L. Burton.*

*A number of railwaymen contacted me
after the deadline for the book had passed, and
although it was too late to include them, I am
grateful that they went to the trouble to get in
touch. I'd also like them to know that when the
next volume of railway memories comes out
they will certainly be included.*

*Finally, a special thank you to Richard
Hardy of Amersham, without whom this book
would certainly have not been possible.*

CONTENTS

INTRODUCTION

Only the very elderly today can remember travelling by steam train when steam was part of everyday life. By the end of the 1960s, the few steam engines that had clung on in odd forgotten corners of the country had gone, although even as they vanished from general use enthusiasts grouped together, determined to save a few engines from the breakers' yard. You don't have to travel far these days to experience again on preserved railways a mode of transport that almost everyone views with great affection. Even those too young to remember when steam ruled the transport system are instantly enthralled by the giant, breathing locomotives that make diesel and electric engines seem somehow tame and inhuman by comparison.

But preserved engines only give us a superficial picture of what steam transport was really like in the days before diesel and electric. There is only one route back into that lost world: through the memories of the men who knew steam transport at first hand; men who drove and fired in cabs open to the worst the weather could throw at them; men who, after the long apprenticeship of engine cleaning and firing, could work any locomotive by instinct. It is the memories of these men that form the basis of this book. But driving and firing, though the best-known areas of steam working, are only part of the story, which is why I have also included the memories of guards and porters, signalmen, a foundryman and a stationmaster. In the steam era each of these jobs was vital to the smooth running of the system.

Courtesy of Milepost 92½ Picture Library

The vast amounts of parcel and newspaper traffic (not to mention passengers) formerly carried by rail meant that the porters – and at a big station there might be a dozen or more – were always very busy. Today the railway is largely a passenger service; newspapers and parcels go by road and the porter's job has vanished.

It was always said that the driver was in charge of the engine, but the guard was in charge of the train. Tucked away in his van at the end of a dozen or more wagons, the guard had to know how to use his brake to keep the train running smoothly; he had to know how to protect his train using detonators, and how to cope in an emergency. He really did 'guard' the train, but like the porter he too is now merely an historical curiosity. Likewise the signalman: he also had an essential role in the old system but his often lonely job, perhaps on some quiet branch line, is now carried out by centralized computers, and hardly a signal box remains.

Many railway books explain the workings of the old system or the way engines were made and run. Other books meticulously list engine types, their names and numbers; yet more discuss railway stations, railway timetables or the process by which the network developed. This book does none of these things. Railway experts will no doubt yearn for more serial numbers or for greater technical detail, but this book does not pretend to be a technical work: instead, it is an attempt to record the personal memories of the drivers, firemen, guards, porters and signalmen who experienced the hardships and happiness of railway work at first hand.

More Tales of the Old Railwaymen covers the memories of ten elderly men who worked in different parts of the country and in a range of different jobs. They have wonderfully vivid recollections of everyday details, and their stories take us back to a vanished world of oil lamps and coal shovels, horse-drawn station carts and smoke-filled engine sheds.

Readers may notice that the details of service differ occasionally from one region to another. In one area a passed cleaner might wear a jacket, in another a set of overalls; in one region the driver might stand on the left of the cab, in another on the right. Variations like these remind us that in the pre-British Rail era the different rail companies really were proud and independent. If the GWR decided to run things in a certain way they went ahead, regardless of anything the LNER or anyone else might be doing. But there was great pride in being an LNER man or a London & Midland man, which is why cleaners – to take just one example – made a special effort when they knew one of their locomotives was on a run that would take it into another region. It is difficult to imagine today's railway employees taking such pride in their work.

Following my successful first book of railway reminiscences, I hope that this second volume, if it does nothing else, gives a balanced picture of the past; a picture that is all the more fascinating for showing us how it *really* was, warts and all.

Tom Quinn, March 2002

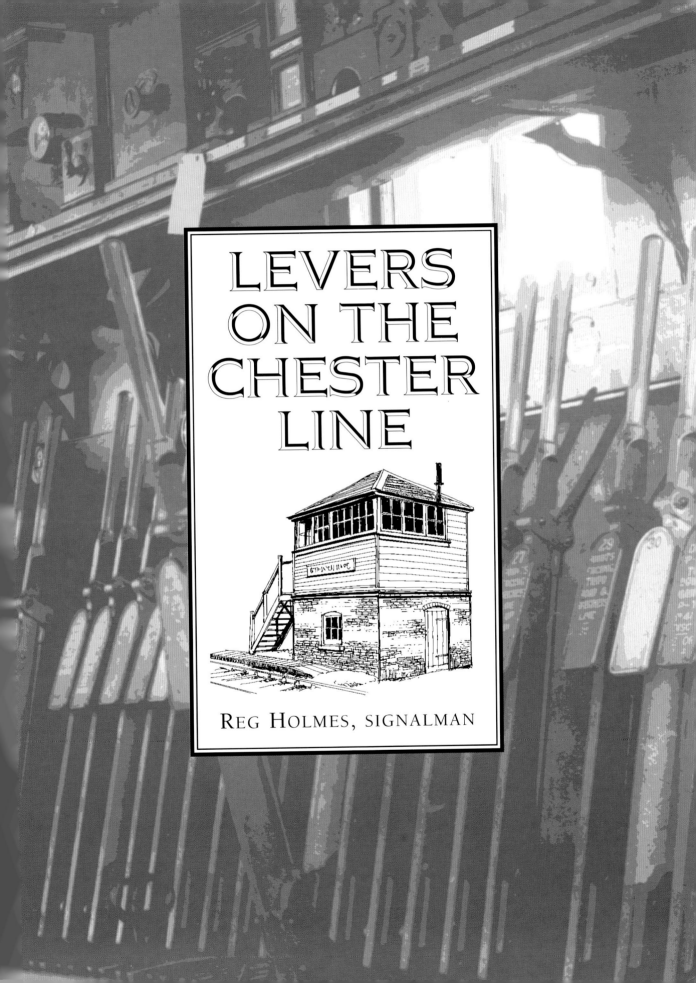

LEVERS ON THE CHESTER LINE

REG HOLMES, SIGNALMAN

've been a vegetarian all my life. My parents were vegetarians, and I grew up in a house where we never ate meat or fish so I've never done it – not once. I've also had lots of different jobs – dental mechanic making false teeth, folk dance caller, farmer, gas worker, postman and cycling hostel owner. The quiet of the signalman's job suited me, although I came to it quite late, in 1950. It must have suited me as I stayed for twenty-six years!'

Sprightly, fit and with a full white beard and bright, inquisitive eyes, Reg Holmes lives in a small, very pretty eighteenth-century cottage that is almost completely hidden – like something from a children's fairy story – in woodland at the edge of Flaxmere Moss in Cheshire.

With its low ceilings, cosy, ancient coal-fired range and walls lined with books and pictures, Ivy Cottage seems an ideal place for quiet retirement. But Reg Holmes has lived here since 1947 and it was from Ivy Cottage that every day, for more than a quarter of a century, he cycled to work through the remote countryside to an equally secluded signal box on the Chester–Manchester railway line (Barrow Fortarvin).

Today, long retired, Reg is animated, lively and remarkably fit-looking for a man who was born in 1913. He spends a great deal of time alone, but admits he was never particularly sociable and that his love of solitude drew him to the signalman's life in the first place.

'Well, it was partly that, but also that I needed a proper job,' he says with a broad grin. 'After I gave up working as a dental mechanic – which I didn't like at all – I tried farming and then, when I came here with my wife, we tried to make a living running the house as a hostel for cyclists and ramblers. I also had a job as a part-time postman, but I was working seven days a week to make ends meet. I enjoyed it, but it was exhausting and we didn't quite make enough money. I'd already tried farming so I couldn't go back to that, so my wife, whose family were railway people and knew about the various jobs that were available, suggested I try working as a signalman. And that's what I did.'

Reg's account of his entry into railway work reflects his remarkably independent spirit. Certainly it must have been difficult for a young man in the 1930s to give up a career in a successful family business – his job as a dental mechanic had been with his father who was a dentist – to go it alone as a farmworker, but Reg was always more interested in doing what he felt he would enjoy than worrying about career prospects or promotion.

'I went farming in North Wales and I loved it but for one thing – I couldn't really reconcile my conscience as a vegetarian with the idea of rearing animals to be killed for food, so I packed it in.

'Then we ran the hostel, and cyclists used to come from as far as Leeds just for the weekend. I remember there was a cycling club called Autumn Tints which always amused me because you had to be over seventy to join, but running the hostel was the sort of life we loved, as many of our friends were ramblers and cyclists.'

Reg is nothing if not stoical about the twists and turns of his long and fascinating life. Having talked to his wife about the railways he enrolled on a six-week course before starting work as a porter-signalman in 1950 at Barrow Fortarvin, a tiny village near Chester.

'Other than what I knew from my wife I had no railway knowledge at all,' he says, before putting an old iron kettle on the hob and then settling into his favourite armchair by the fire in the little sitting room.

'I passed all the tests after six weeks, which was apparently pretty good going because most signalmen I knew started out as porters so they knew a bit about the running of the railways before they started to learn formally, as it were, about working in the signal box.. Despite my lack of experience it wasn't difficult to get in – I think the fact that the war had ended only a few years earlier meant there were manpower shortages across much of the railway in this part of Cheshire. I was in the slightly odd position of going straight in as both a porter and signalman. I worked in the box when there were trains, but in quiet times – and there were plenty of those – I worked on the platform, issuing tickets, sorting out the luggage and so on.'

Reg emphasizes the enormous responsibility of the signalman in those early days, but the basis of the training was knowledge of the regulations and the rule book, as he explains.

'The regulations were for the signalman in particular; the rule book was for railwaymen, whatever their specific job. But as a signalman it wasn't just a question of knowing the regs – you had to stick to them whatever happened because you had the lives of a train full of people in your hands. Just one slip and the train might be off the rails or into another train. The regulations for the signalman were complicated and lengthy, but it was a bit like being in the army – if you knew the regulations really well you had no need to be afraid of anyone.'

Reg's first signal box had been built as early as 1850. It had an old cast-iron fire pot where the signalman could cook his breakfast. Some twenty-nine levers operated signals on the main line up to $^3/_4$ mile away and on the sidings.

'At first all I remember is what an awful lot of shunting there was to do – in those days so much freight that now goes on the roads went on to the railways. We had timber from the forests round here, and a lot of farm produce and lime, and the whole lot was shipped out of our area via the sidings at my box. We had a big warehouse in the sidings with the train going in empty at one end and out at the other full.'

One of Reg's abiding memories is of the staffing levels at country stations in the 1950s. At Delamere (where he worked later) there was the stationmaster – 'He was like a god!' – two clerks, two porters and three signalmen, one for each shift.

'And of course there were the platelayers keeping an eye on the track in a way that no one bothers with now, which is why we have these terrible accidents. Yes, I remember there were three platelayers and a ganger patrolling the line regularly between the signal boxes, checking the ballast under the rails and checking the rails themselves for cracks or other signs of damage or wear and tear.

'They walked the track every day whatever the weather; every inch of it was looked over. Somehow I don't think the system today can match that – mind you, that isn't saying much as there doesn't seem to be any kind of system at all today!'

The age of steam seems less remote than it really is when one listens to Reg, who manages to evoke not just the railways and the men who worked on them with him, but also the sense of a world before the dominance of the motor car. Because the railways were still Britain's most important form of transport well into the 1960s, whether passengers or freight were being moved around the country, the system had to be kept in tip-top condition. More than a century of railway experience had decreed that high levels of manning were essential to prevent accidents and to ensure the smooth running of a system that was the envy of the world. That level of manning later came to be seen as excessive, but, as Reg insists, had more to do with saving

Reg fills in his logbook on a hot summer's day

money than with improving safety or efficiency. Of course there were quirks in the old system, and quirky characters who didn't quite run things according to the strictest interpretation of the rules.

'I found that out right at the start,' says Reg, 'in my first signal box. There I was, ready to get started, when the stationmaster appeared. I can still remember his name – it was Harry Burton and he was one of those immaculately dressed, ramrod-straight types. He said "It's Reg, isn't it?" "Yes, Mr Burton," I replied – the boss in those days was always "Mr so and so". "I've heard a lot about you," he said, "and I've come to tell you that I like my bed." For a minute I wondered what he was on about, but then he went on. "I don't want you calling me out of that bed unless it's absolutely necessary."

'The point of the thing was that the signalman was supposed to call the stationmaster out at any time day or night if there was a problem, but I think Harry Burton must have thought I could manage well enough on my own because the next thing he said was, "Don't get me out of my bed, and in return I'll do a Nelson and turn a blind eye." He was really saying he would trust me to get on with the job.

'But I thought it was funny because after this long, serious chat he said, just as he was about to go, "And I do like a cup of tea when I come to sign the book."

'That was something vital in the old days – record keeping. You had to make a note of every train movement in a big book and that book had to be signed for and verified by the stationmaster.'

At this point Reg leaps up and darts towards the boiling kettle. He is remarkably agile, despite a serious accident which put paid to his motorcycling days when he was eighty-eight. As he makes the tea he explains that he remembers nothing about the accident, but that after several days in hospital he made a full recovery and was able to return home.

'The only problem now,' he says with a smile, 'is transport. But I'll just get my old pushbike out and I'll be able to get to the village and shops.'

Much of the safety of the old railway and its systems was based on the culture that successive generations of railwaymen inherited. The stationmaster would make a shrewd assessment of his signalman and know whether or not he could rely on his integrity and ability. If he could – as in Reg's case – then he knew that the man could be relied on in a crisis. But backing up the inherited culture of safety was a written record that was meticulously kept.

'Oh, that was rigidly adhered to,' explains Reg. 'When the signalman accepted a train from the next signalman up or down the line he made a note of the time, and he would also note the time he handed the train on. Those books were kept for years. Their evidence was admissible in a court of law. That's how much care the system took.'

In these days of automated signals and centrally heated offices it is very difficult to imagine what it must have been like when the signalman arrived at his box on an icy morning in January. 'It was very uncomfortable,' says Reg. But there were compensations.

'Well, usually when you arrived your mate would have got a fire going and there was enough heat – well, just about – to cook up a bit of breakfast. The biggest problem we had was the lack of coal. It was a sort of standing joke that the regulations stated that the signalman was entitled to 1lb of coal per hour during winter. You can imagine how long that lasted – about ten minutes! It was hopeless, but the way we got round it was to hold up a big lump of coal as a train passed. The driver would see it as he went up the line and then later on when he came back down the line he'd drop off maybe half a ton of coal – that was more like it!

'We used a fire pot to keep a kettle hot for tea. It was a sort of cast-iron pipe a bit like a chimney pot and you lit some coal in it and put your kettle on top – took bloody ages to boil!'

The complex system of bell signalling, that allowed trains to be passed from one signal box to the next as they completed their journeys, was one of the wonders of the old railway system. A signalman might be accepting trains continually and as he did so he would know, from the next signalman's signal, what kind of train – passenger or freight – it was.

'I'll give you an example of how it worked – as the train passed the next signalman's box up the line on its way to me, the signalman would give two on his bell. I would give two bells back to say I'd heard and understood. Now, I would want to be rid of that train as soon as possible to the next signalman along the line so, if I could, I would immediately signal to the next box and so it would go on until the train reached the end of its journey.

Inspecting the complicated signals apparatus

'In the steam days safety was always paramount – we lived and breathed safety – and it was rare for any attempt to be made to short-circuit the system if there was any chance that it would weaken watertight systems.'

Occasionally, of course, it did happen, and despite the gap of more than forty years the memory of one such incident still angers Reg.

'Sometimes when you were single-line working – it might be just the down line because the up line was being repaired – the bosses would ask you to allow trains through when the man in charge of the work was absent. This wasn't allowed because the line not under repair might have been fouled by a piece of machinery or whatever from the line being worked on. Only if the man in charge of the work was with you could you accept that the line was OK and trains be permitted through. Once an inspector tried to make me allow single-line working when the man in charge of the repairs was not around. I said I wouldn't do it and the driver waiting to go through agreed with me, but still the inspector reported me. I would have liked to have seen his face when he heard I was congratulated by someone much higher up for sticking to my guns!'

Though always a stickler for the rules when it came to safety, Reg occasionally found ways round some of the more annoying aspects of railway bureaucracy. When what he calls the 'pinstripe bosses' began ringing him two or three times every hour just to ask if everything was OK he pulled the plug on the phone.

'Well, it was making the job impossible – I was supposed to be concentrating on the trains, not on someone in a suit miles away from the action!' he says with a broad grin. 'When someone complained later that they couldn't get through I shook my head and agreed with them about how unreliable the phones were.'

It was an excellent system, but even high levels of manning and great attention to detail couldn't prevent every accident. Reg remembers seeing trains pass his box with flames a yard long shooting out of their wheels – 'the brake linings were on fire' – and that meant an immediate signal of seven bells to the next signalman. Seven bells would make sure the train was stopped and either repaired or taken out of service. On other occasions a piston rod or some other part of the motion work might have come loose, or something would fall off a goods train and foul the line.

'The problem with these things, but particularly fires in the brake linings, was that the driver wouldn't easily be able to see them. That's why the golden rule for the signalman was to watch every train carefully as it passed his box.'

Like most signalmen Reg got on very well with the drivers because they relied on each other, and the drivers had to call at the signal box regularly to sign on.

'This happened when a train couldn't be offered immediately to the next signal box up or down the line. If the driver had to stop his train at your box he would jump down, come in the box and sign the book to say he was here at a certain time on a particular day. That way there was a written record when he had to account for the fact that the train was late. In those days being late –

losing time – was really upsetting for a driver because they prided themselves on their timekeeping. Many of the old drivers knew the road so well they could keep perfect time without bothering about a watch.'

Reg remembers only a few derailments in his twenty-six years. Usually they were caused by objects on the line or by wagons that were 'buffer-locked'.

'What used to happen was that two wagons would meet and their couplings would lock together but in an awkward way. This meant they were "buffer-locked" so the truck couldn't turn and it would drop off the road. As soon as that happened all the stop signals would come on.

'Another problem which arose more often than you'd think was a runaway train – by that I don't mean that the driver had lost control of the whole thing, but that a wagon at the back of the train had come unstuck and was rolling back. We had a special signal for that because there was no way you could stop it. You just had to let everyone know what was happening and keep everything else out of its way. One detonator meant, "Look out, something unusual"– three meant "Stop!"'

Other hazards included wires from the signal levers breaking or seizing up in extremely cold weather. When that happened a platelayer or a porter might be co-opted to stand at the appropriate points with a green flag and plenty of detonators to put on the track to warn approaching trains – not an enviable job on a day when temperatures might never rise above freezing.

'The detonators were the only thing we had in fog – if a driver drove over a detonator and heard the explosion he knew he had to stop because there was some blockage up ahead.'

As Reg describes what was clearly a well-oiled and rehearsed system it is easy to forget just how physically arduous the railwayman's job could be in those pre-electronic days.

'Well, I think people would be surprised, for example, at just how much effort it took to pull on the levers that operated the distant signals. Just the weight of the wire on a signal $\frac{1}{2}$ mile away took some shifting. I think the best way to pull involved getting your weight behind the lever rather than using brute force, but it was definitely an art that took some time to acquire. I remember when the late Poet Laureate John Betjeman visited my box as a guest of the district manager. He was very keen on the old railways and he tried to pull one of the distant levers. He couldn't do it at all. He was one of a number of VIPs who visited the box now and then – I remember him as a very friendly chap and interested in everything.'

During his years in the signal box Reg saw something that few signalmen would ever have seen. He happened to be looking down the line when to his astonishment he saw a signal arm simply fall off and crash down on to the track. He had to run out on to the line waving a red flag to stop the oncoming train.

'That was really unusual. Most of our problems involved sleepers falling on the line from passing repair wagons, or farm animals straying through fences. Also, I remember finding a number of dead hares on the line. As meat was still rationed in the early 1950s I picked them up for a friend – couldn't eat them myself of course.'

Reg's passion for books is evident from the number of titles on the shelves that line his cottage, and even in the signal box he found time to read. He studied languages and read widely during quiet times at work. And when as a trainee porter-signalman he wasn't signalling or reading he helped out at the station – painting the white lines at the edge of the platform, keeping the station clean and tidy, delivering parcels to nearby houses. If one of the other signalmen was in the box Reg would stand on the platform checking the trains in and out, shouting out the name of the station as the train arrived, and then making sure all the doors were properly closed as it departed.

In 1951 Reg moved from Barrow Fortarvin, the porter-signalman's box, to a full-time box at Cuddington a few miles further off, but still on the old Chester line. This was some 10 miles from his home, so when he found that the Delamere signalman lived at Cuddington he did a swap. That way the Cuddington signalman was close to his home and Reg was close to his.

'Swapping like that was quite common,' he recalls. 'We were both signalmen at the same grade so it wasn't a problem. My new box was lovely and warm and I used to look forward to getting into it on cold winter's mornings after the ride there on my bike. I liked it so much that I stayed in it for the rest of my career – right up until I retired in 1976. I could have moved on several times. I was offered promotion, but that box at Delamere – now long gone – was close to home and I was happy there.

'We took turns on the shift, three of us – you had to do a week on 6am–2pm then a week on 2pm–10pm and finally 10pm–6pm. It messed your sleeping patterns up, but after a while you got used to it.'

It was the sense of being independent that Reg loved most about the Delamere box. Once he'd arrived and taken over he was in sole charge, and would be left largely in peace until his relief arrived eight hours later. The other signalmen enjoyed this too: one used to shoot rabbits from the box and then cook them for his lunch. But for Reg one of the great pleasures of the box was that his wife could join him for a mid-morning cup of tea while waiting for the train to Chester. It was a serious and important job but with a human edge to it.

And there were moments of fun and great humour, too.

'A driver stopped and climbed up into my box one day. He said, "What kind of a bloody line is this – I've stopped at every box for that slow train in front. In the first box I saw the signalman making a canoe, in the second box the signalman was

mending a clock, in the third box he was making a beehive, and here I find you playing the mandolin!"'

But railwaymen didn't all get on well. Reg was always aware that there was friction between some drivers and guards.

'Yes, they used to play tricks on each other. The driver would know when the guard had a pot of tea on his little stove in the brake van and he'd deliberately stop or slow down suddenly to tip it off. Then the guard would get his revenge when the train was going up a hill by just screwing down the brake a little to make it hard or even impossible for the engine to get to the top. If the train stopped and the driver lost time he'd get what we called a "Please explain" notice.'

One of the more fascinating aspects of the signalman's job was the elaborate nature of the procedures for single-line working. In Reg's box, when training at Mouldsworth, there was a large key with a big ring attached to it. This would be held out by the signalman as the train passed his box. The fireman on the engine footplate would put out his hand and try to get his arm through the ring, thus carrying off the key. Once he had the key no other train could be on that section of line.

'But the most interesting aspect of the key business is that three signalmen in three different places had to simultaneously wind an electric lever in order for the lock to open and the key be released. Again it's an example of that culture of safety which once existed but is, I fear, now gone forever.'

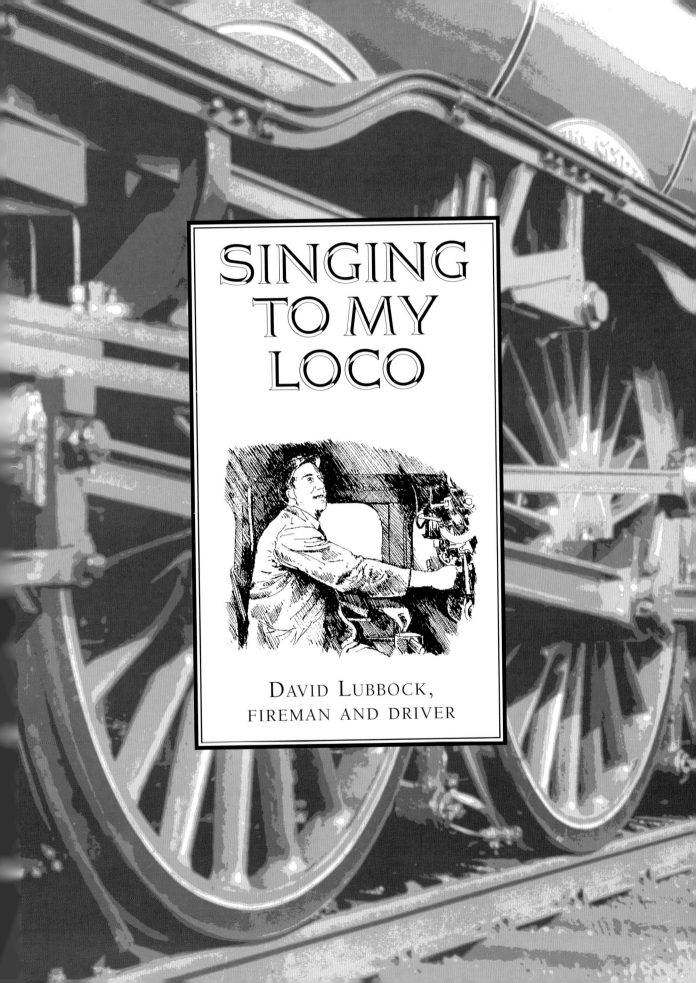

SINGING TO MY LOCO

DAVID LUBBOCK,
FIREMAN AND DRIVER

David Lubbock remembers every detail of his more-than forty-year career on the railways as if it had all happened yesterday. He is as fascinated by the railways now as he was in 1945 when he started work, aged fourteen. It was just a year after he had left the little village school in Briston, near Sheringham in Norfolk. Through the last years of World War II he'd watched the bomb-carrying trains pass close to the village on their way to the big American bases, and he remembers watching a German air attack on the railway junction at Melton Constable a few miles away.

'They hit the water tanks at the rail junction there. The Germans were always trying to disrupt the rails to stop us moving things round the country. But it was a funny thing – we saw an enemy bomber get shot down and it turned out that the German pilot had been chosen for the mission because he'd gone to school in Norfolk and knew it like the back of his hand!'

David is a remarkably animated figure who looks a good deal younger than he is – he was born in 1930 – and has some wonderfully well-preserved mementos of his railway years. These include a driver's food and toolbox dating back to before World War I, and a beautifully preserved railwayman's lapel badge and fob watch from the 1920s.

As well as his clear recall of the war and long-vanished steam, David has vivid memories of the era of horse-drawn transport and of the old-fashioned harvest at which he first saw the girl who was to become his wife.

'Yes, I met her when we were harvesting together as children. All the local kids helped with the harvest and I can remember seeing her as we worked on the threshing machine. We travelled about and did all the harvesting on local farms. I don't think the threshing machine gave me a taste for steam trains, but it was a fascinating piece of equipment,' he says with a smile. Then he helped his father, who worked with a team of men building airfields for the United States air force.

'My dad put in the first runway fog lights ever used – we thought they were a marvel. But he knew that most of the local work was in farming, and since he didn't want me to get stuck with that he insisted I apply for a job on the railway. He was friendly with the shedmaster at nearby Melton Constable, Tom Sands, so that was where I started as an engine cleaner aged just fourteen.'

David insists that at that time to have much chance of getting a job on the railways you really had to know someone on the inside.

'A lot of people wanted to work on the railways because it was reliable, steady work, so it wasn't all that easy to get in. Also, there was a lot of deference in those early days – seems incredible now, but you still had to put "Your humble, obedient servant" at the end of your letters!'

David was quickly sent from Melton Constable to work at Norwich, and the first thing that struck him was the state of some of the freight on the wagons.

'I couldn't believe it. When I looked in one of the trucks on a bomb train I found the shells hadn't been packed carefully, or even put in boxes. No, they were just chucked in any old how like bricks, but they were piled up to the roof – thousands of them. We were convinced they'd blow up any minute!'

Like most young men at the time David was also dazzled by the sheer number of Americans in East Anglia – 'You just had to put your hand out of the window and you'd touch one!' he says with a grin. But he was also amazed at how well off they were compared to the locals; they seemed to throw away vast amounts of almost new equipment. David collected scrap American ammunition boxes, which could be found all over the place, together with huge numbers of spare parts for bicycles.

'We salvaged tons of bits and pieces out of the trucks – all of it had been discarded by the Americans who just seemed to have too much of everything. We used to paint their old ammo boxes and use them to carry our kit, instead of the metal boxes we were given by the railways. They seemed better made, and like everyone we thought, "If it's American it must be worth having".'

By 1946 David was a passed cleaner for firing. 'Even cleaning locomotives for just a year taught you a hell of a lot about how they worked,' he says. What had in an earlier age taken perhaps as long as six years to achieve now took only a year. The combination of manpower shortages and men absent doing their National Service had overturned the lengthy system of promotion by seniority.

For the young boy starting out as a cleaner, firing must have seemed a long way up the ladder, but the ultimate prize – driving – was still a long way off. David remembers in great detail the excitement of his first day's firing. His driver was Billy Girling.

'Oh, I remember Billy well. The cleaner lads thought he was a god; we thought all the drivers were gods because they were so far above us, and if they didn't behave like gods they certainly acted like lords of the manor! Billy looked me up and down with a very sceptical eye and said he didn't think I was up to it and didn't want to take me, but the foreman convinced him and by the skin of my teeth I was on the footplate at last. I think I must have done all right that first time because Billy was very pleased, and to please a man of his experience was a big thing. He was in his late fifties then, with two sons, both drivers.'

In 1948 it was David's turn to do his National Service. The railways were no longer a reserved occupation as they'd been in the war, and David found himself in a spartan training camp in Farnborough, then still a small town in the Hampshire countryside.

'It wasn't too bad because they kept all us footplate men together. It wasn't deliberate policy – the authorities had pounced on the railways so thousands of railwaymen were starting their National Service at the same time.'

David was trained as a railway clerk, which has always seemed slightly odd to him given his experience of more practical railway work, but after a few months he moved from the Army Railway Depot to a big holding camp near Aldershot.

'Next thing I was told I was going to Kenya – well, I think it was Kenya – to help with a groundnut scheme of all things!'

In the weeks leading up to his departure David seems to have been constantly on the move. He spent some time in London, and was then taken to Liverpool. Sailing on the *Empire Pride* he was sick all the way to Gibraltar, then enjoyed the journey immensely until they reached Port Said in Egypt. He was still with a dozen fellow railwaymen and together they were assigned to the movement control section of the Railway Engineers at the railway station and docks at Port Said.

'My job was sorting out the paperwork for the movement of troops. I was also one of the very few people in the army who had a British passport issued by the British Consul at Port Said. This was because one of my duties involved going on board ships that had arrived at Port Said and collecting diplomatic parcels. This was about the time that things were getting very nasty as the state of Israel was established and I remember hearing gunfire all night which was pretty terrifying. I'd never been anywhere like this before, and I only got out of it when I was sent to Tripoli a few months later to relieve a chap called Geoff Bird. I remember his name because we became friends and I discovered that he came from Parkeston here in Essex close to where I live now, although at that time of course I didn't know I'd end up spending so many years here. His father was a guard on the trains at Parkeston Quay.

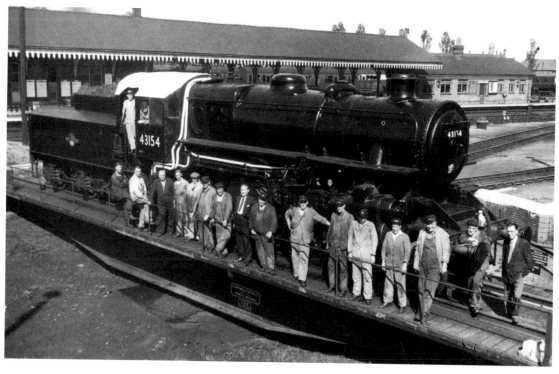

A Standard engine at Melton Constable in the 1950s

'I spent two Christmases abroad, and was finally demobbed in 1950. I remember arriving in Southampton aboard the *Eastern Prince*, spending a night in London, and then getting the train back to Norwich to stay with my future wife's family.'

On 27 March 1950 David was back firing on the footplate for a weekly wage of £5 10/- (£5.50p). 'They had to take you back and you kept your seniority,' he recalls, 'but by this time the old LNER had been nationalized. I remember we had to put British Rail signs on top of the old LNER ones.'

In the same year David married the girl he'd met at harvest time. They held their reception at the Railway Institute at Melton Constable, but David knew that if he was to get on he would have to up sticks and move elsewhere. So, a few months later, he and his wife set off for the rail depot at the port of Harwich on the Essex coast.

'I came as a fireman and there was some resentment at us youngsters among the older drivers and firemen because for our age we held pretty senior positions. Because of the war and National Service I'd been driving trains at the age of twenty-two, which – strictly speaking – was illegal according to Board of Trade rules, so I had to go back to firing. But I was a passed fireman – passed, that is, for driving – in 1953, on 6 May to be precise. It was the day the Harwich–Hook of Holland British Rail ship *Duke of York* was cut in half at sea by the American ship *Haiti Victory*, with the loss of eight lives.'

From then on whenever there was a vacancy – someone ill or away on holiday – David stopped firing and became a driver. 'Well, they often picked me because I'd fired for most of the old boys and I knew the road, the details of the various routes, like the back of my hand. On my arrival at Parkeston depot in 1952 I started firing with Whitley Hazleton on a B1 class 1226. He really took me under his wing, and our months together were among the happiest of my whole career.

'I was now in the old MGN region, which we always called the "Muddle and Get Nowhere Railway", but since Parkeston was near the port of Harwich we were dealing with troop trains a lot of the time, and they were run in a far more sophisticated way. The thing I remember most about driving was the noise. I could keep my eyes closed and always tell where we were by the sound of the engine. I never got it wrong, that's how well I knew the road. But like most of the drivers I didn't have a watch – didn't need one. Keeping time was all a matter of experience.'

Working in fog was the worst experience of all for David, and he recalls the terrifying day he had to climb a signal gantry in conditions so bad that he couldn't see his hand in front of his face. Extremely cold weather could also be dreadful for driver and fireman, with the footplate permanently open to everything the weather could throw at them. But he came across all kinds of different problems during his time on the road.

Drivers and firemen at the Melton Constable social club in the 1950s

One of David's most treasured possessions: an early driver's watch with specially thick glass for extra protection

'I can remember once the road into the Stratford loco shed was blocked with engines with a detonator behind each. Conditions were so bad you couldn't see a thing and we were all working blind. We went over the detonator and eased on to the engine in front, but no one from the shed would come out and help us so we had to leave the engine where she was, making the traffic jam even worse. It was all mechanical in those days: no electronic aids, no sensitive computer-operated systems. Everything was done by eye and hand and when conditions were atrocious everything stopped. The only way to prevent collisions was to put small explosives on the tracks to warn the driver that there was another engine ahead.

'Then there was the old roster system – nothing like it now. The top link – that meant the most senior drivers and firemen – worked on the passenger trains. In passenger gangs you had what were called nominated engines, which had two sets of men to one engine. You'd always hide your good tools in case the man in the other team damaged them or lost them.

'Next down the ranking came the goods link and then the shunting link. The premier link was on the express trains – they were the crème de la crème. They worked all the express trains to and from Liverpool Street. But a passed fireman like me got any and every fill-in job that was going.

'Firing was very tiring until you got used to it, but it kept you fit and we were young then. On some trains you'd be shovelling almost continually. On others you'd get plenty of time to pause between bouts of activity. A lot of it had to do with the driver – with a really good driver there was less firing to do because you used less coal. With a poor driver you'd get through several lorry loads!

'A good driver would use what was known as pulling up the lever or wheel, which shortened the piston travel and superheated the steam – that meant you were really using the steam. Some drivers just opened the regulator and you'd get spinning wheels, sparks and a lot of wasted power. For that sort of driver you had to work really hard as most of your effort went up the chimney!'

Over the years David drove a great many different engines – Bongos, Britannias, old shunting engines, standards – but then he was always keen to gain experience.

'All engines are different – like women, we used to say! When you're firing on an engine you quickly learn which ones need more fire at the front of the firebox, and which need it at the back. Some needed a thin fire, others a much broader-based fire. With some engines it was always murder to make enough steam, but I was very

David during his National Service. He was sent to Egypt with the control section of the Railway Engineers

pleased one day when the shedmaster said to me, "Why can you make that engine steam when others can't?" I didn't know the answer, but I had a sort of feel for coaxing life into her. I can't remember what sort of an engine she was, but she needed an unusually shallow fire. Even now I can't tell you why it worked, but it did. Maybe I was taking the advice of old Whitley Hazleton. "When the chips are down," he used to say, "sing to your engine" – which is what I did.

'I lived near the loco shed in those early days and the shedmaster knew I was hungry for money so he made sure he put plenty of work my way. He'd always knock me up when someone was needed. I lived in rooms before I got a railway cottage.

'For a while in Melton Constable back at the beginning of my career I was what we called a "knocker-up". I'd be given a list of names and addresses, and for each one there would be a different instruction: it might say, "Knock on back window for so-and-so", or "Rattle the drainpipe", but whatever it was you had to knock or rattle till the man was awake and had *told* you he was awake. Usually they just grunted or shouted out the window. If you disturbed a neighbour or upset a dog you had to scarper quickly!'

Shift work, early hours and often arduous conditions never dented David's enthusiasm for the railways; but it wasn't all hard work.

'We had good fun too. I remember at Melton Constable I used to fire for a driver called Aubrey Dent, and when we were working the trains that went through the royal estate at Sandringham he used to slow the train down and I'd jump off and take a few pheasants or rabbits out of the gamekeepers' snares. Meat was still rationed at that time so it was a welcome addition. Once I jumped off and nearly failed to get back on. I ran like mad and just caught the guard's van at the back!'

But as the 1950s wore on change was inevitable, and the long-established systems of the steam days – that had proved their worth over more than a century – were soon to be overturned by the arrival of diesel engines. The long years of the driver's apprenticeship were soon discarded because almost anyone could learn to drive a diesel engine in a matter of weeks.

'The biggest upset I can remember was when the diesel engines first came in. We had some of the earliest in East Anglia, around 1954 or 1955, built by the Drewry Car Company. The older steam men hated them and many never got the hang of driving them, but for us youngsters they were like a new toy. They were used for shunting only, at first, because they weren't man enough for the heavy train ferry wagons.

'By this time I was working at Dovercourt, the Harwich docks, and the train ferry wagons were the heaviest wagons on the railways – they needed the sort of powerful diesel engines that just weren't available then. The early diesels overheated easily and we just had to make do until they gave us 350hp English Electrics and GEC Blackstones. Eventually British Rail had all kinds of diesels – there was no standard. I passed for driving on mainline diesels in 1960, which was quite early when you think that in some areas steam didn't finally disappear until the late 1960s.

'We were sent to Ilford, I remember, to learn all about these new-fangled machines. We went in groups of six for a fortnight. That's all it took – just two weeks, compared to years on the steam locos. We were with drivers in their sixties who found it all very difficult.

'I used to sing songs to the old steam engines, but there was no point with the new diesels. They didn't have any character and there was no skill involved in driving them. You didn't have to coax them – you just threw a switch and they worked.'

One of the curious things about David is that he always liked to be as smartly dressed as possible, even when he was cleaning and, later, firing and driving.

'I always wore a white collar and tie with a safety pin across the tie. They got pretty filthy but I thought it was important,' he says with a huge grin.

Like most steam men, David always had his favourite engines and his eyes light up when he recalls their individual characteristics.

'I reckon the best steam engines I ever worked on were the Britannias – used for passenger work mostly – and the worst were undoubtedly the K2 Ragtimes used for mixed traffic, either passenger or freight. The Britannias gave a lovely smooth ride, while the Ragtimes were rough as anything.

'Some of the goods trains were only part-fitted with vacuum brakes. Where the last half wasn't fitted with vacuums, I'd try to fit my own. I'd just walk along adding vacuum pipes to the wagons that didn't have them. That meant I could run faster and

stop quicker. On the goods run to Spitalfields market the signalmen at Kelvedon and Witham used to shout, "It's Lubbock – let him go!" I think I had a bit of a reputation!

'The shunting engines we used were Hunslets – they had a gear stick like a car and when we were shunting we'd always try to get the job done quickly so we'd have time for a game of cards. We'd put the engine in first gear, which would allow it to push the wagons on to the buffer stops. Then we'd jump off to help the other shunters coupling up. When the engine had shunted into position on its own the engine would cut off and the brakes would apply. That way we'd be done a lot quicker. It didn't always go as smoothly as that – once when the line was really greasy I let the engine do the shunting on her own and she knocked the buffer stops over so her front wheels went off the road. Everyone said, "Oh, you're in trouble now", but I got some scaffolding poles that were lying around nearby, put them under the wheels, and – with the luck of the devil – ran the train back up them on to the rails.'

By 1962 David had driven every steam and diesel engine then in service in the area; he'd been a local ASLEF representative for years and at a time when unions and management were often at loggerheads he'd managed, together with other representatives, to maintain a good relationship with the bosses. But despite his increasingly prominent position he was still surprised when

David the proud driver: always smart in collar and tie

he was appointed running foreman at Parkeston at the age of just thirty-two.

'Going from passed fireman straight to running foreman was unheard of in those days. It was also embarrassing in lots of ways because I was suddenly in charge of many of the men I'd been firing for and they were a lot older than me. But I think they were OK about it in the long run as I managed to bring lots of work to this area. Our trains went from here to Ely, Peterborough or March, as well as London. Whatever rosters came up I could always say I had men who knew the road. I loved being supervisor at Parkeston – I was in charge of 100 sets of men and thirty locos.

'When diesel came in we built a diesel maintenance shed with platforms and huge green double doors at either end. The doors caused a bit of a gaffe, which I must admit was all my doing. I can remember it as if it was yesterday. Sid Peace, an Ipswich man, was marshalling the locos – getting them in order – but he was having problems shuffling the steam engines in such a way that he could also get a diesel loco in, so I said, "Leave it to me". I told him I'd get a spare 204 Hunslet shunter and pull the steam locos with that.

'Well, I got a row of engines on and started moving. I should just add that the big green doors at the end of the shed had just been repaired after someone drove an

A group of firemen and drivers circa 1954: David is second from left

The railway football team: David is standing, second from left

engine into them. They'd only been up a week and along I came; because someone hadn't pinned them back I went straight into them with my row of engines and down they came again.

'I got what we called a "number one" – that meant a disciplinary note. I was accused of breaking the doors down with a steam loco. At my hearing I thought I'd be all right because the charge sheet they'd filled out said I'd knocked the doors down with a steam loco, whereas I'd actually done it with a diesel. So on that basis I denied the whole thing. They were outraged, and when they insisted that it was obvious I'd done it I just repeated that I hadn't done it with a steam loco, which was what the charge sheet said. The shedmaster was getting very hot under the collar by this time and suddenly announced that he'd fill out another charge sheet, but I knew the rules and told him he couldn't just change the charge like that. He was so cross he told me to get out, but that was the last I heard of it.'

The old loco shed closed in 1967 to make way for a new container terminal, and David was told he might have to move to Colchester. He went to see a friend in shipping services for whom he'd done a few favours in the past. The friend, Archie Mackey, found him an old shed in the port area – really more of a garage – and David moved his men in and avoided both the forced transfer to Colchester and a lot of redundancies.

'We kept as many men as we'd had before because there was plenty of work on

the diesels. You couldn't do it now, of course. Once they decide to shut you down that's it, but in those days we set up independently and the management decided it might be worth keeping us after all, so they did.'

In 1969 David became yard master in charge of all the shunting for Harwich Shipping and International Services. Eventually he became chief dock supervisor, and then West Quay manager. It was all a long way from those early days cleaning engines.

'Very few men went from cleaner to one of the management grades, but despite the fact that I was well paid at the end I still say my best days were on the footplate. There's nothing like it and although it's now gone forever, I'm glad I was there.'

Asked if he has any regrets, David says only that he left school so early. He finally retired in 1987 when the train ferry service from Harwich closed.

Funeral train

In the early 1900s Tom Holton's father was stationmaster at Towcester, and the family lived in the station house. When Tom's sister died in an epidemic, the railway company put on a special train to carry the coffin and mourners to their ancestral home at the village of Slapton 5 miles away.

The train waited at the nearest point to the church while bearers carried the coffin ½ mile along a field path to the churchyard where the burial took place. The track was a single line so no other train could pass.

The family were then conveyed back to Towcester.

The train company, the Stratford-upon-Avon & Midland Junction Railway, was more than once in the receiver's hands, but it was not too poor to pay this compliment to a faithful servant.

The Railways of England, W. M. Acworth, 1889

A town's decline

At the formerly flourishing village of Hounslow in Middlesex so great is now the general depreciation of property on account of the transfer of traffic to the railway that at one of the chief inns is an inscription, 'New Milk and Cream Sold Here', while another announces the profession of the occupier as 'Mending Boots and Shoes'.

Hounslow Courier, 1842

The greatest mystery

In the early hours of 13 October 1928, a Bristol-bound freight train, a passenger train from Birmingham and an empty fifty-wagon train collided near the village of Charfield, at that time still in Gloucestershire. Dozens of people were killed, including two children. A terrible tragedy by any standards, but also the beginning of one of the greatest of unsolved mysteries, for the two children who died have never been identified.

The railway company insisted the two children had not been on the train and that the two small bodies actually belonged to two strays who'd been sheltering under the railway bridge at the time of the crash. But the driver of the passenger train survived the crash and spoke up. He explained how he had waved to the two well-dressed children when they boarded the train at New Street, Birmingham. He had noticed them – the girl aged about eight, the boy eleven – because they were unaccompanied and without luggage.

Legend has it that for years after the crash an elderly woman in black, driven by a chauffeur, visited the grave at Charfield where ten victims of the crash – including the children – are buried. After the war she ceased to come and there is no evidence anyway that her visits were not to remember one of the other victims. As each year passes there is less chance of identifying the children and the story remains one of the greatest of all railway mysteries.

Railway England, J. Fisher, 1935

Memories of the earliest railway

In 1831 a Mr Fergusson of Woodhill, Edinburgh, travelled from Manchester to Liverpool by rail, a mode of transport then in its infancy. His account of the journey, originally published in *The Agriculture Quarterly*, is a rare first-hand account of how rail superseded coach travel.

'Having formerly visited the manufactories of Manchester, I proceeded without delay to Liverpool, by the far-famed railway. We started with eight carriages attached to the engine with such imperceptible motion, that it was only when I found myself unable to read a milestone, or to distinguish the features of those who darted past in the opposite direction, that I was led to consult my watch for the rate of travelling; when I found, to my surprise, that the next 5 miles were done in fifteen minutes; nor was it possible, from the precautions so judiciously taken, to feel either anxiety or dread.

'From the powers of the locomotive engines on the railroad, goods and passengers are conveyed from Liverpool to Manchester, a distance of 32 miles, in about two hours. As a contrast to this rapid transmission between the two towns, the following statement may not be out of place. A stage coach was first established between Liverpool and Manchester in 1767. The roads were then so bad that the coach was drawn by six, and occasionally by eight, horses, and it required the whole of the day to perform the journey.

'An old gentleman, now resident in Liverpool, relates that, between fifty and sixty years ago, he occasionally visited Manchester, when the coach started early in the morning from Liverpool; the passengers breakfasted at Prescot, dined at Warrington, and arrived sometimes in time for supper at Manchester. On one occasion, at Warrington, after dinner, the coachman intimated his anxiety to proceed; when he was requested by the company to take another pint and wait a little longer, as they had not finished their wine, asking him at the same time if he was in a hurry. "Why," replied John, "I'm not partic'lar as to an hour or so."

'Among other regulations, a watchman perambulates every ½ mile to detect any stone or other dangerous impediment upon the rail. As he sees the carriages approaching, if there is a difficulty, he stops and extends his arm in sufficient time to enable the engineer to stop the train. Some accidents undoubtedly happen, but they may be traced, in almost every instance, to a want of ordinary prudence and attention in the unhappy sufferers.

'As we bowled along, a little circumstance, more ludicrous than dangerous, occasioned a small loss of time. The hook by which No 2 carriage was attached to No 1 suddenly gave way, and the engine, with one carriage only, shot off like lightning, leaving the others to follow as they best could. The alarm was, however, quickly given, the engine reversed its movement, while our impetus carried us yet steadily forward, and the whole affair was speedily adjusted.

'The tunnelling and cutting upon some portions of the line are stupendous, and the whole stands a magnificent sample of enterprise and scientific skill.

'The consternation occasioned among the coach-proprietors who had formerly served this route, was of course great, and heavy individual losses necessarily incurred, with much jealousy and ill-will towards the intruder. A knight of the coaching days, who had been forced to drop his reins, mustered up resolution one morning to take a trip by the railway, and, in spite of a very reasonable stock of indignation, soon felt his asperity giving way under the excitement of such a slapping pace, and, ere he had proceeded far, exclaimed in ecstasy to the engineer, "Come now, my lad, that's it, do boil up a bit of a gallop".'

History of the English Railway, J. Francis, 1851

Credit: National Railway Museum/Science & Society

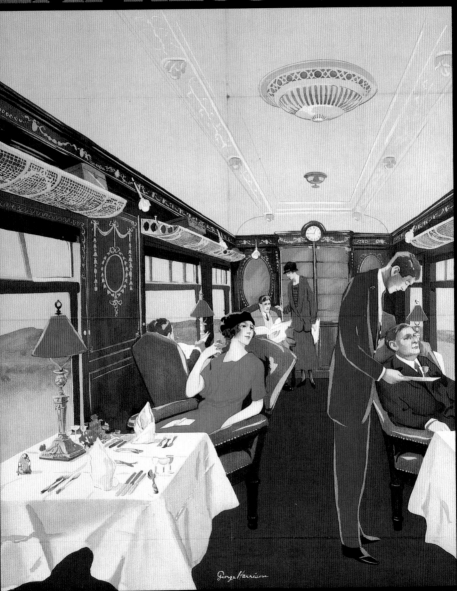

LONDON & NORTH EASTERN RAILWAY
EXPRESS EASE

THE "HARROGATE" PULLMAN
LIMITED TRAIN
Between KING'S CROSS (London) and
LEEDS in 3½ hrs. HARROGATE 4 hrs. RIPON 4¼ hrs.
Also DARLINGTON and NEWCASTLE

BOOK YOUR SEATS IN ADVANCE AT

LEEDS		LONDON		HARROGATE	
	Telephone		Telephone		Telephone
Leeds Central Station (Booking Office)	21725	King's Cross Station (Enquiry Office) North 4200		Harrogate Station (Booking Office)	
Leeds City Office, 141 Briggate	24683	59 Piccadilly, W. 1 - - Regent 3437		Harrogate Town Office, 16 James Street	155
		71 Regent Street, W. 1 - - Gerrard 6663			
		87 Gracechurch Street, E.C. 3 Avenue 560			
		Savoy Hotel (Booking Office), Strand, W.C. 2			

Published by the London and North Eastern Railway Company.
Adams Bros. & Thardlow, Ltd., Printers, London and Leicester.

A tunnel to Old Nick

Robert Stephenson's rail tunnel to Liverpool's Lime Street station was dug in the 1830s. Like all early tunnels it was dug entirely by hand and mostly by Irishmen whose grandfathers had dug Britain's huge canal system a century and more before.

As the men dug and hacked ever deeper in the appallingly hot, badly lit and entirely unventilated system, they noticed that the ground beneath them was beginning to move. The men stood back quickly focussing their dim lights on the place. Minutes later the tunnel floor gave way and the navvies were horrified to see below them shadowy figures and dim lights moving. They ran screaming from the tunnel convinced that they had broken through to the devil's own kingdom.

In fact Stephenson and the other engineers involved in digging the tunnel had no idea that another tunnel was being dug in the same area – tunnel depth and trajectory calculations were then in their infancy so bumping into unexpected things was quite common. But in this instance it took several hours to convince the men that they were not in fact about to be carried off by Old Nick. The other tunnel was being dug by Joseph Williamson, an extremely wealthy retired tobacco merchant, who built miles of tunnels and caverns under the Edge Hill district of Liverpool in order to provide jobs for unemployed men.

The Railways of England, W. M. Acworth, 1889

Beecham gets sick

Sir Thomas Beecham was travelling in a non-smoking compartment on a train belonging to the Great Western Railway. A lady entered the compartment and lit a cigarette, saying, 'I'm sure you won't object if I smoke.'

'Not at all,' replied Beecham, 'provided that you don't object if I'm sick.'

'I don't think you know who I am,' the lady haughtily pointed out. 'I'm one of the directors' wives.'

'Madam,' said Beecham, 'if you were the director's only wife I should still be sick.'

Great Railway Stories, 1902

Stage coach decline

The whole of the stage coaches from Glasgow to Edinburgh are now off the road, with the exception of the six o'clock morning coach which is kept running in consequence of its carrying the mail bags.

The Glasgow Courier, March 1842 (two years after the opening of the Glasgow to Edinburgh railway)

Bag man

A traveller entered a railway compartment containing a lot of luggage strewn over the seats, but with only one occupant, a young man in the corner seat. The incoming passenger was preparing to make himself comfortable in another corner seat, but was informed that the bag which was placed there belonged to the young man's friend, who would be along in a minute.

The newcomer therefore took a seat alongside the bag. No one appeared and presently the train commenced to glide out of the station. As it started he lifted up the bag and gently dropped it out of the window, remarking benignly: 'Well, your friend won't want to lose both his train *and* his bag!'

Our Best Railway Stories, 1900

Drinks for all

A country stationmaster having a grievance which was unable to get righted locally, took it to headquarters. Calling on the chief superintendent, he gave him a long-winded account of his troubles. He had completely exhausted the chief's patience by the time he commenced again going over the whole

ground, and the superintendent politely told him he could do nothing in the matter. This failed to satisfy the aggrieved party, who began the whole story for a third time, with the result that he was ordered out of the office. The superintendent, being only human, may also have given him his 'blessing'.

Still obsessed by a sense of injustice and dissatisfied with railway superintendents, the stationmaster by some means got access to the sanctum of the general manager, who, having heard something of his plaint, asked his why he had not gone to his superintendent. 'I've already been to him, sir,' was the reply. 'And he told me to go to the devil. So here I am.'

Our Best Railway Stories, 1900

Appendix

Every railwayman engaged in the movement of traffic is supplied not only with the railway company's book of rules and regulations, but also with a more hefty volume called *The Appendix to the Book of Rules and Regulations,* or more familiarly the 'Appendix'.

The latter is the guards' and signalmen's *vade mecum,* and applicants for both these positions have to know something of its many provisions which outline the course of action to be taken in a railway working emergency. These books, together with uniform clothing, hand lamp and other equipment supplied by the company, have to be returned when a railwayman leaves the service.

Some time ago one who had been dismissed had failed to surrender the whole of his equipment, and he was requested by letter to send in his 'Appendix' forthwith. Whether he wilfully misconstrued the

IN THE SIDINGS

request is not clear, but he replied: 'I've lost my job and sent in my uniform. I don't mind being unemployed so much, nor being unclothed, but I'm hanged if I'm going to be operated on for all the railways in the kingdom!'
Our Best Railway Stories, 1900

Why bother with the East coast?

Competent observers were, however, convinced that all the lines it would pay to construct were already made. For instance, it was gravely argued that the Lancaster and Carlisle (a line that in fact paid enormous dividends for years before it was absorbed into the North Western) would 'prove a most disastrous speculation'.

It was evident, said the wiseacres, that it could never have any goods traffic; and as for passengers, 'unless the crows were to contract with the railway people to be conveyed at low fares', where could they be expected to come from? The through traffic could be conveyed almost as expeditiously and far more cheaply in the 'splendid steamships which run to Liverpool in sixteen or seventeen hours from Greenock'. As for the rival East Coast scheme, 'this most barren of all projects, the desert line by Berwick', was even more fiercely assailed:

'A line of railway by the [East] coast,' writes one gentleman, 'seems almost ludicrous, and one cannot conceive for what other reason it can have been thought of, except that the passengers by the railway, if any, might have the amusement of looking at the steamers on the sea, and reciprocally the passengers by sea might see the railway carriages.

'The improvements that are constantly taking place in marine engines and steam vessels,' writes another correspondent, 'are so great that there cannot be a doubt but they

will soon attain an equal rate of speed to the present railway locomotives.'

For all that, the East Coast route was strongly advocated, and an influential deputation, headed by Hudson and Robert Stephenson, had an interview with Sir Robert Peel at the Treasury to solicit Government assistance to the project.

The construction of the High Level Bridge at Newcastle, as a single line to be worked by horses, was under consideration. Speaking of the proposed Caledonian line from Glasgow and Edinburgh to Carlisle, the *Railway Times* writes in January, 1843, that, if, in any way the present attempt should 'be rendered nugatory, the next ten years will not see the commencement of a line to Scotland by the West'.
The Railways of England, W.M. Acworth, 1889

Mrs Busybody

'But what are your duties on the railway?' asked Mrs Busybody of a man at station. 'Well, mum, it's this way. You know the bloke wot taps the carriage wheels wiv' his liddle 'ammer. Well, I'm 'is mate. I 'elps 'im listen.'
Our Best Railway Stories, 1900

Flying steam carriage

The entire unconsciousness even of the railway men themselves of the revolution they were working is nowhere better shown than in the different methods that were proposed for conducting the traffic. Practically, the locomotive, as we have it today and capable of working up to 1,000 horse-power, was already there. The multitubular boiler and the steam-blast had long been in common use. But neither the public nor the specialists were convinced that the right system had been hit upon. To say nothing of a 'patent aerial steam carriage

46

which is to convey passengers, goods, and despatches through the air, performing the journey between London and India in four days, and travelling at the rate of 75 to 100 miles per hour', all kinds of substitutes for locomotives were being sought for.

One day the *Globe* reports that a 'professional gentleman at Hammersmith has invented an entirely new system of railway carriage, which may be propelled without the aid of steam at an extraordinary speed, exceeding 60 miles an hour'. Another day the Edinburgh & Glasgow Railway have, says a Scotch [sic] writer, 'the discernment to employ Mr. Davidson, a gentleman of much practical knowledge and talent', to construct for them an electro-magnetic carriage. The carriage, 16 feet long by 7 feet wide, was duly placed upon the rails, and 'propelled by eight powerful electro-magnets about a mile and a half along the railway, travelling at the rate of upwards of four miles an hour, a rate which might be increased by giving greater power to the batteries, and enlarging the diameter of the wheels'.

'The practicability of the scheme is,' we are assured, 'placed beyond doubt,' and its 'simplicity, economy, safety, and compactness render it a far more valuable motive power than that clumsy, dangerous, and costly machine the steam-engine.'

Then, again, Messrs Taylor and Couder, C. E., patented an ingenious system by which a carriage was to be drawn along the line 'by the muscular power of the two guards who constantly accompany it'. The system, which is at the present moment in use for towing purposes on many German rivers, the Elbe for one, required that an endless rope should be laid along the line, and wound on to a drum which was attached to the carriage, and made to revolve by force, manual or mechanical, supplied from inside the carriage itself. Next Mr England, the engineer of the London

& Croydon Railway, made a manu-motive railway carriage, 'very light and elegant in appearance, and capable of carrying seven or eight persons at the rate of 18 miles an hour'. 'We have no doubt,' says a railway newspaper, 'that these machines will come into, general use, as they will effect considerable saving to the company in time expense of running an engine.'

The Railways of England, W. M. Acworth, 1889

Drinks for all

The day was hot, and as the train drew up at a station a warm-looking old gentleman put out his head and asked the guard if there was time to 'have one' at the refreshment rooms.

Credit: *National Railway Museum/Science & Society*

The reply was in the affirmative, but he still seemed concerned lest the train might start without him. 'Oh, that'll be all right,' said the guard reassuringly, 'I'll just step in and have one with you.'
Our Best Railway Stories, 1900

Missed

PORTER (*to distressed passenger*): 'What's the matter, sir?'

DISTRESSED PASSENGER: 'I-missed-that-bless-ed train only by-half-a-minute.'

PORTER (*disgustedly*): 'And you're making as much fuss as if you'd missed it by half-an-hour.'
Our Best Railway Stories, 1900

Early electric

In nothing appertaining to railways have the last ten years seen a greater change than in the progress of electric traction. The mileage of electric tramways in the world today is some-thing like 15,000 miles. On railways proper, in London, Liverpool, Chicago, Budapest, and other places, scores of millions of passengers per annum are being carried safely, speedily, and conveniently by electric energy.

At Baltimore, goods trains of 1,500 tons are being hauled over very heavy gradients by the same force. Tens of millions of pounds are being spent in the construction of electric railways in London, Paris, Berlin, and other great cities. The conversion from steam to electricity of the underground lines in London, and of the elevated lines in New York, is practically settled, while in Chicago the work is already done. Ten years hence it will probably be quite the exception to find a steam locomotive employed in urban or suburban passenger service. But, as far as can be judged at present, the employment of electricity in ordinary medium or long-distance railway service, either for passengers or goods, is not likely to come within the range of practical politics just yet.
The Railways of England, W. M. Acworth, 1889

Third class on the railway, Epsom Races, 1847

THREE
GENERATIONS
ON THE LNER

ALLAN RICHARDSON, FIREMAN AND DRIVER

The railway is in Allan Richardson's blood. His grandfather was the running shed foreman at Grantham, starting work in 1893, and his father was a fitter who'd begun work at the end of World War I in 1918. Allan was born in 1923 just a short distance from the running shed, and he spent his working life moving up and down the vast network of railways that served London, the north-east and the wide, flat lands of East Anglia before the Beeching cuts of the 1960s.

'From the earliest I can remember I always thought I'd work for the railway,' he says now. 'I couldn't wait to leave school. Every day at the school assembly they used to read out all the jobs that those over fourteen could apply for and as soon as I could, I applied. Mind you, it could all have been very different because I actually went for two jobs when the time came, one as a junior reporter on the *Grantham Journal*, the other as a messenger lad at Grantham loco shed. With my background I was bound to get in the shed.'

Allan was right: he was delighted when, following his interview at the shed, he was asked to start work.

'It's odd, but most of us old railwaymen can remember the exact day we started work – for me it was 30 March 1937.'

Allan is the first to admit that the fact that his dad worked as a fitter in the shed helped enormously, but the messenger lad's job was nothing to write home about.

'It was a grand name for an office boy, and I got just 16/- [80p] for working a forty-eight-hour week, but it was better than school and I didn't have far to travel each morning as the shed was just up the road from where we lived.'

Allan had just about settled in to his new career when his father got the mechanical chargeman's job at Newark, 14 miles away.

'Mum and dad moved to Newark and I went with them, but still keeping my job at Grantham. This meant I had to travel to and from Grantham morning and evening, which was a very long day for a fourteen-year-old. I left home at 7.30am, arriving back at 6.30pm, Monday to Friday, and 7.30am to 3pm on Saturdays. I gave mum 2/6d [12½p] a week on top of my board, to pay for my season ticket, so not much was left out of my 16/- a week.

'At Grantham I spent my days in what would now seem an incredibly Dickensian office – there were tall wooden clerks' stools in rows behind sloping wooden desks, gas lamps, ink pens and ink wells, and of course everything there was done by hand. Most of my time was spent despatching letters and writing out the clock cards for the men. It was important that they were done regularly because at the end of each week

they were sent to the accounts office so the men could be paid.'

Allan was working for the Great Northern section of the London & North Eastern Railway, whose head office was Peterborough. He was a messenger boy at Grantham until December 1939, by which time the outbreak of war had changed everything.

'That was the year my father got the shift mechanical foreman's job at Peterborough and we moved again. Men were being called up and there were shortages of staff everywhere, which is why, once again, I was very lucky. My opposite number at Peterborough – a lad called Charlie Carter who was two years older than me – got called up and I was offered his job.'

Allan was just sixteen when the family moved to Peterborough. Officially he was in what was known as the technical department, though he was still graded as a messenger.

'I didn't mind about that because I was on the princely sum of 25/- [£1.25p] a week and the work was more interesting. I was looking after the locomotive records. Everything that happened to an engine was recorded: maintenance and repair on valves and pistons, tender tank cleaning dates, and so on. At the end of each month I also made a list – a blacklist, if you like – of all the work that should have been done but was outstanding.

'You wouldn't believe that old office. Apart from the usual rows of clerks' stools and desks – the same here as in Grantham – there were three fires. One right next to the boss, one for the chief clerk, and one between the three messenger boys.'

Allan was in the office at Peterborough until he applied for a job as a cleaner. He was successful and started work on 13 May 1940.

'My main motivation was money, although even then every boy really wanted to be an engine driver. I was paid 6/- [30p] a day as a cleaner, but if I got a firing turn it was 9/6d [47½p] a day – and bear in mind that a labourer at that time earned a good bit less than that.'

Allan's dominant memory of his time cleaning engines is of the singing among the lads and the pranks they played on each other.

'There was one trick we all played on someone at one time or another. We would have one of the lads in the cab and another at the back of the tender. Then, by lifting off the vacuum pipe at the end of the tender and placing it in a bucket of water held by another of the conspirators, as soon as someone walked past in front of the engine the one in the cab would open the large ejector on the brake valve. The water disappeared out of the bucket and came out of the chimney, then descended in a shower of black rain and soaked him – it was called "giving the elephant a drink". But we used to sing all the music hall hits of the day and we got on very well because we'd started work pretty much at the same time and were all roughly the same age.

'The job was pretty straightforward. We used what we called purr, a sort of cream, to do the actual cleaning, and we were given a specific amount of time to do a specific engine. You really did have to complete the job in the time given. For an A3 Pacific, for example, we were given twenty hours – that meant a gang of five working for four hours. For V2s and 02s we had sixteen hours. Our approach to cleaning was to work well, but as fast as we could so we got the job finished early. We could then spend the rest of the time having a fag or playing cards. The older men called our gang "the Ovaltinies" after a famous radio advertisement of the time.

'We called the lad who cleaned the cabs "the front rubber", and though that might

Climbing out of a 4-6-0 locomotive firebox circa 1936: cleaning was one of the dirtiest jobs on the railway
Credit: National Railway Museum/Science & Society

sound cushy compared to cleaning the motions, it wasn't because the cabs got filthy – the coal dust and soot from the lighting up process would be all over the place, some of it hanging down in great lumps almost like bunches of grapes. Sometimes we'd be given as many as sixteen engines and told just to clean their cabs. The quickest way to start was to put the injector on and use the slacker pipe to hose the cab down and get rid of the worst of the dirt that way. If the chargeman caught us doing it this way he'd kick up a bit of a stink, but we did it if we could get away with it – it may not have been thorough, but at least it looked clean!

'We gave the gauge glasses where you checked the water level a more careful clean, but you have to remember we were only given half an hour to do each cab so we couldn't treat them like the crown jewels.'

It was common, explains Allan, to be given a whole series of engines that needed only cab cleaning, or wheel and motion cleaning, or just boiler and tank cleaning, but despite the dirt and the shift work – as a messenger he had been used to a regular 8am–6pm working day – he was in his element.

'It was completely different from office work. You felt you really were on the railway at last, and although we were proud of what we did people did get up to tricks. For example, we weren't allowed to clean an engine if it was wet or what we called "sweaty" – that meant it had come into the shed from the cold, and condensation had formed on it. You could usually spot the level of water in an engine tender tank from where the line of condensation ended. Anyway, you couldn't clean an engine in this state because your purr would just smear everywhere – if we were feeling a bit mischievous we'd sometimes deliberately wet the engine so we didn't have to clean it!'

Courtesy of Milepost 92½ Picture Library

'I'd been cleaning for just four weeks when I saw the inspector to see if he would let me start firing. He asked me a lot of questions to see if I knew the rule book, and lots of technical stuff: did I know how to put the injector on, did I know how to prepare the engine, did I know how to coal and water it, and did I know how to dispose of an engine. Disposing of the engine meant knowing how to throw out the fire.'

After the requisite number of firing turns – each one meticulously recorded – Allan's pay was increased to 9/6d (47½p) per day whether cleaning or firing. A cleaner might average only one firing turn a week, or one a fortnight, so it might take a number of years to reach the requisite number of turns, which represented one year's work, not including Sundays. Curiously, no one seems to know why Sundays were not included in the calculation. When the required figure had been reached the cleaner received a black cloth jacket in honour of his new status.

Having passed all the necessary tests, after 626 firing turns, Allan found himself earning the fabulous sum of 10/6d (52½p) a day. But that was for firing days. On days when he was cleaning he still earned 9/6d.

A driver explaining the valve gear of a 4-6-2 gauge Princess Royal class steam locomotive to a schoolboy circa 1938. Credit: National Railway Museum/Science & Society

'We were so keen to learn how to fire that from day one as a cleaner we used to practise on the stationary engines. We'd show each other how to swing the shovel because there was an art to it. If you got into a rhythm it wasn't so tiring. The first engine I fired on was a J52 in Spital Yard at Peterborough. Early firing turns were never on the main line – just in the shed or on the shunters.'

But, as in other regions, the war had created curious anomalies on the LNER. With so many men having been called up Allan found himself, at just seventeen, firing for a sixty-five-year-old driver, who had been asked to stay and who should have retired.

'You've got to remember that drivers were only one step down from God so far as we were concerned. If a top-link driver spoke to you you'd almost bow before you replied! So I was very nervous on my first day on the shovel. I knew the driver would be watching my every move, and drivers could be harsh if they thought you weren't up to it. A driver didn't want too much smoke, and he didn't want the engine blowing off steam because you'd built up too much pressure too soon. I remember one old boy shouting at me, "Don't do that now – I'll tell you when!"'

The statistics behind firing a steam engine say a great deal about the strength and stamina of the men who did this arduous job. Allan estimates that you would use 45lb of coal and 40gal of water per mile on average, and all that coal had to be shifted by the fireman. Like so many firemen Allan found a shovel he liked and stuck to it.

'I don't know why it worked for me, but it did, so I used to hide it every night under the breakdown train! A fireman's shovel has its own special design and they varied from region to region. They used to say it took four men even to lift a Great Western shovel! But generally speaking shunting shovels were short-handled, while shovels used on the big main-line engines had long handles so you could get the coal well into the back corners of the firebox. This was particularly important on the Pacifics because most of the coal was burned in the corners. We used to say that the best firemen kept the coal dancing on the firebars.'

Most of Allan's early firing was on what were called transfer trips, moving freight wagons from one yard to another. The huge Fletton brickworks were not far from Peterborough and much of the traffic was bricks, together with agricultural freight.

'I got a bit bored at this time, I must admit,' says Allan. 'I always seemed to be going up and down the same bit of track!'

But then, in 1941, it was time for another change. Allan's grandfather retired and Allan's father took over as running foreman at Grantham.

'It was like musical chairs – we were all off back to Grantham again! I went back as a passed cleaner and discovered that there was a real shortage of men. By 1945 I'd done my firing turns and I was a regular fireman, but Grantham was in a bit of a state after the war. Manpower shortages were so bad that main-line drivers and firemen on the long journeys north couldn't get back in time to have twelve hours' rest before they started work again on their next shift the next night. Twelve hours' rest was a legal requirement, so where in the past they would only have used fully made-up drivers and firemen they had to use passed firemen and passed cleaners to drive and fire and fill the gaps. The old seniority system had changed enormously, and we were all moving up much faster than ever would have been possible in the pre-war days.'

Allan is absolutely insistent that rapid promotion through didn't compromise safety, but with little investment in the track, embankments and so on during the war years there were some nasty moments.

'One Sunday we had a special from Grantham to Doncaster. I was firing for a driver called George Chantrey on a passenger train. The signals were off when we got to a place called Grove Road, which was just before a sharp bend. We shot round that bend and saw right in front of us that the level-crossing gates were down. George put the brakes on, but it was too late – we knocked one gate flying, and got the second gate mangled in the buffers and carried it along with us. The effect of it dragging as we carried on was incredible: ballast came up into the cab like machine-gun bullets. We were lucky though because no serious damage had been done – just a broken headlamp – and using the coal hammer we were able to get the gate off the front of the train and continue on our way. We carried on to Retford loco shed to get a replacement headlamp. We put the lamp on the front of the train, carried on to Doncaster and never heard another word about the incident. It was strange, though – manpower shortages were so bad that when I went into Retford loco shed to get that replacement headlamp, there wasn't a soul there. I couldn't find anyone to ask if I could have the lamp, so I just jumped up on an engine and took one.'

Grantham was bombed during the war, and Allan still has a paper knife made from part of a German plane shot down during a raid on the town. When the war ended manpower shortages gradually eased, and by 1951 Allan was firing in number one link, the London to Newcastle trains. He remembers with particular fondness a few of the old engines, but the A1s were his favourites.

'What I liked about the A1s – and I don't want to get too technical here – is that they didn't have what was called conjugated valve gear. Conjugated valve gear had been invented by a man called Sir Nigel Gresley. His system meant that two outside valves on an engine drove the middle valve, but the fulcrum pin and bush of the middle valve wore quickly and this meant the system didn't stay true – it got out of sync. This meant a jerky engine performance. The A1s, on the other hand, didn't have this system – on the A1s each valve had its own eccentric which meant they stayed in sync and you had a better locomotive where the valves were always true.'

By 1954 Allan was passed for driving, so he had to come off the main line and was back working on the shunters.

'You had to start at the bottom again because you'd gone from being a fireman with a lot of seniority to being a driver with none. When I fired on the main line I'd been paid an extra hour's pay for every 15 miles worked beyond 140 miles. On the long main-line journeys, such as King's Cross and return to Grantham – 210 miles – I'd get twelve-and-a-half hours' pay. This was good money for a fireman. Back on shorter journeys as a driver this all stopped and I got paid less as a result.'

During firing turns on the main line Allan had been rostered with the same driver for many years. Together they worked what were known as the Parlies – Parliamentary trains, so called because they stopped at every station. Allan

remembers the King's Cross to Grantham Parlies as 'rotten jobs' because they stopped at twenty stations on the way and the journey seemed interminable.

'The reason they still ran these Parlies was that in the early days of the railway an Act of Parliament was passed which stated that every station in the country had to have at least one train stop at it at least once a day. A lot of trains were still run just to avoid breaking the law. When I first started firing on the Parlies I used to fill up the firebox and my old driver would then let me drive while he just kept an eye on things. It was completely unofficial, but it was really good training.'

In 1957 Allan applied for a regular driver's job at King's Cross. He had enough seniority, having started cleaning in May 1940.

'Seniority lists were posted up at all depots. When you got a list of jobs you checked your seniority and if you were above the seniority date given for a job you could apply. The whole seniority system came in about 1900 because in the early days a driver might choose a fireman who'd only been working for a few months just because they were mates. This could mean that another man who'd already been waiting for years would have to wait even longer while he was passed over by younger men. At least with the seniority system everyone was in the same boat.'

As Allan was based at King's Cross he came to live in London. He enjoyed the responsibility and drove both freight and passenger trains, and still admires a system that had a century of safety practice behind it.

'You had route cards and you had to sign to confirm you knew every road, or you could say you needed a refresher course on a particular road, or even cross a road out if you no longer felt happy that you knew it. And you received a book each week with the temporary speed restrictions on various roads. This – the Permanent Way Notice – was and still is known among the men in the Yorkshire area by its nickname: The Navvy. That name probably hasn't changed in more than a century and it refers to the fact that it was the navvies who built the permanent way – the track, embankments and bridges.'

The driver's routine seems to have been pretty much the same whichever region he worked for. Allan remembers how his friends used to be puzzled by his start times.

'Sometimes we'd have a start time of 6.27am. That sounds odd, but the reason for it was that you had one hour to prepare your train – that meant oiling everything, trying your injectors, checking your coal and water – and fifteen minutes to get your engine to the train. That start time of 6.27am was chosen so we'd be ready to take out the 7.42am, exactly one hour and fifteen minutes after we signed on.'

In Allan's day no time was allowed for tardy staff. If the footplate staff were late for a particular job the foreman would pick another set of men. Late trains were to be avoided at all costs.

'This is the problem today – there's no back-up. The rail companies are so keen to put their shareholders first that they won't pay for back-up. If there's a problem they just cancel or delay the train. That never happened in my day because the passenger was the first priority.'

But however carefully considered, the various rules were occasionally ignored. Allan remembers working the *Flying Scotsman* to Newcastle, and then picking up the *Heart of Midlothian* for the journey back. The inspector came along to Allan's cab and reported that there were fourteen carriages weighing 468 tonnes. Allan immediately protested because he knew that the train was not permitted to exceed thirteen carriages and 450 tonnes.

'As soon as I said that, as cool as you like the inspector looked down his list and announced: "Fourteen on, 449 tonnes." And that was that.'

Firemen and drivers were generally a good-hearted bunch, and Allan remembers with particular fondness an old driver's announcement when he was six weeks away from retirement. 'I've had a good time, let someone else have the engine.' Having said that he jumped off the footplate and asked to spend his last six weeks back in the loco shed.

'There were a lot of what I suppose you would call old characters among the drivers. I remember it was a regular joke about a driver I worked with for years that he'd get black in a flour mill. Within minutes of getting in the cab he'd have filthy hands which he'd then wipe all over his face! We used to say that was why we never got the Royal Trains – and lot of Royal Trains came through Grantham. You always knew them; they were the only trains allowed to travel with four headlamps.'

In Allan's time you were very lucky if you were driving by the time you were thirty. Today, as Allan points out, it's quite common to be in your early twenties. 'We call 'em "boil in the bag drivers"!' he says with a smile.

Things changed dramatically for Allan in the late 1950s when the first diesels came in. He'd been secretary of the Grantham Railwaymen's Mutual Improvement Classes and was asked if he would instruct on diesels. He was sent on a five-week

course and only ever did three days driving after that. He became acting inspector and was soon passing men out on diesels.

'We had to learn on what were called Mirlees Brushes, but every diesel engine was different so men had to learn each separately. On the old steam engines when you knew one you knew them all. I remember we once had to take over an American engine at Grantham in the dark and it was as easy as riding a bike, even though we'd never seen an engine like it before.

'People complain about diesels, but change was inevitable. Diesels were cleaner and more efficient, and even I'd noticed that towards the end of the steam era the old wonderful Yorkshire coal we'd used was always in short supply. The skill did go out of the job because the diesels did it all for you, but people often underestimated them. I remember being with one old driver in a diesel cab and when I told him he needed to start braking in order to stop at a station he said, "I was driving when you were still in nappies." That might have been true, but I was right and he couldn't stop in time. With diesels you had no sensation of speed and people often underestimated how long it would take them to stop.'

The last steam engines on the LNER disappeared in the mid-1960s and the old locomotives were sent off to a huge breakers' yard at Norwich.

By 1962 Allan had gone into the time and motion department at King's Cross. He was to stay for five years but hated it – 'My years in the wilderness!' he now says. He escaped in 1967 and became head office locomotive inspector at London's Liverpool Street station. Then, after two further promotions, in 1981 he became chief train crew inspector at York. He retired in March 1986, forty-nine years to the day after starting work in that little office in Grantham.

'THE GUARD IS THE MAN...'

ARTHUR ARCHER, FOUNDRYMAN AND GUARD

The Great Western Railway made everything – engines, wheels, pistons, coaches and carriage cloth. We also made our own soap, pins, grease, furniture – everything. We ran our own buses, foundries and even coal mines.'

Arthur Archer is proud of his forty-two-year career with the GWR. His working life is also an illustration of the range of railway jobs he so eloquently describes. Arthur started his career by applying (unsuccessfully) to work as a French polisher for the GWR and ended up, via the footplate and the foundry, as a guard. In a fitting tribute to a man who typifies so much about one of Britain's greatest railway towns, Arthur was also to become the 100th mayor of his home town, Swindon. The very first mayor of Swindon had also been a railwayman.

But being mayor must have seemed light years away when Arthur's father, who worked as a labourer in GWR workshop No 7, put his eleven-year-old son's name down for the works.

'When the great day came for me to start work,' says Arthur, 'I went down to Parkhouse for a medical and an aptitude test. It was the first year of World War II. I thought it would just be routine and then I'd start my apprenticeship as a French polisher, learning to get the wood ready for the carriages, but I failed the dictation test. The general manager called my dad down to get me, and when I got home I got a terrific hiding because dad had lost pay for the short period during which he'd waited to be told that I'd failed. He was a very hard man like that.'

A remarkably robust-looking man despite several heart attacks, Arthur is also unusually direct and honest about railway life in the 1930s and '40s. He remembers how men were sent home for three days with no pay if they were late for duty twice; how pay was deducted for the least infringement of the rules; and how strict was the split between various jobs, both socially and professionally.

'You had money deducted for the smallest mistake – even going to the loo for too long! And whatever your apprenticeship you were always sacked when you were twenty-one anyway because it reduced your period of continuous service and saved the company money when and if you were re-employed, which you usually were. Then there was what we called the War Wages. All pay rises for cleaners, firemen and drivers since the Great War were not part of basic pay – they were extras and calculated on the basis of a rate of pay that, obviously, hadn't changed since 1918. Again, it was a way of keeping the workers' pay as low as possible because only your basic pay was taken into account when it came to calculating pensions.'

But there was also a sort of rigid caste system on the railway. Footplate men would never mix with porters or signalmen, and even if two men happened to know each other socially they would always address each other formally if they met at work.

'You also asked permission to enter a signal box or to get up on the footplate. It was just an unwritten rule of respect,' says Arthur.

A couple of years after failing to start as a French polisher, Arthur, aged sixteen, took the test again and passed, but this time he'd applied to work as an engine cleaner. 'That was hard old work – our chargeman used to come round with his white handkerchief and wipe it on the pistons. If there was any oil or dirt on the handkerchief we had to do the whole job again, and we often did have to. We used to say that the chargeman brought the dirt with him!'

On night shifts Arthur and the other boys would take it in turns to cycle round Swindon knocking on drivers' doors to wake them.

'We'd knock 'em up an hour before they were due in, but that was a miserable job in the cold with only faint oil lamps on the bike and not a soul awake anywhere.'

When the lads weren't cleaning or waking up the older men they sat in the old brick cabin with its long wooden benches and searingly hot cast-iron pot-bellied stove. 'We'd doze in the cabin or play cards, but one or other of the lads – usually another cleaner – was always dropping detonators down the chimney. We lost several stoves like that! They quite literally blew up when the detonator went off. Mucking about, pranks and plenty of jokes meant that, despite the unsocial hours, being a cleaner was fun.'

After seven months' cleaning engines Arthur became a passed fireman. He was sent to Cardiff for a medical, and then to Bristol to learn the regulations.

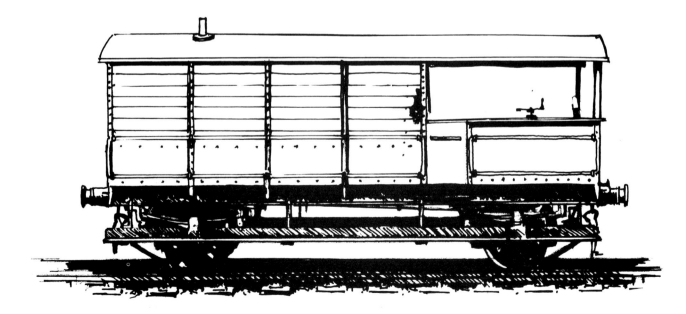

'I took the rule book with me everywhere – mind you, sticking rigidly to the rules could make things very slow and inefficient. If you broke the rules and everything was all right, nobody said a word, but if you broke the rules and something went wrong you were in very serious trouble indeed.'

Arthur fired for six years but disliked it. After the fun of cleaning engines, firing was hard, isolated work, as he explains.

'It wasn't being on the shovel that was the problem – it was little things like trying to break the ice on the water bag at 2am some freezing January, or running tender-first in sleet in December. We had open cabs on the GWR and the wind could take the skin off your face.

'Then there were the strict rules. For example, most of the engines I fired on were governed to 240lb per square inch. That was your running pressure. If it got above that the engine would blow off to ease the pressure, but if that happened at a station you were in trouble. This was particularly frowned on at Paddington because it was a completely covered station. The rule was that you should have just enough steam to assist the brakes as you came into the station, but you really used the handbrake.

'Apart from upsetting passengers with the terrific din, the problem with blowing off steam was that the force of the blast actually damaged the paintwork on the station roof. There were strict rules for running and strict rules for dealing with drivers, too.

'There's no doubt that life in the 1930s and '40s was more rigid and formal than it is now, at least so far as having respect for your elders is concerned. This was partly because in my day you would probably only pass for driving when you were well into your forties. After all those years and all that effort to get to the top you didn't want some newcomer talking to you as if you were just one of his mates.'

After his six years on the shovel Arthur left to join the army, a move followed by tens of thousands of others caught up in National Service. He was sent to Kenya and then Libya, teaching locals how to operate machinery of various kinds. By 1955 he was married and back in Swindon.

'Swindonians are a funny lot – grumpy and tight-fisted,' he says with a smile, 'but much as they may complain about the place they stay put and when they go off for a while as often as not, like me, they come back again.'

Back in Swindon, Arthur got a job in the GWR foundry as a machine moulder, making the moulds that were used to produce brake blocks. 'They were solid chunks of iron and as you can imagine the GWR got through a lot of them.' Two years later he left the railways completely for a few months, only to find something pulling him back.

'I tried other jobs but couldn't settle to them, so I went back and worked in No. 21 shop where the carriages and wagons were made, and then in No. 23 shop cutting up old wagons. This was skilled work because we were under instructions to take certain parts out complete and undamaged so they could be used again. Eventually I went back to the foundry, but whatever I did I found it tough – all railway work was hard then, and I always found it difficult having to do long hours of overtime to make a living wage. You could go for weeks without seeing daylight.'

It was a major accident and the scandal that followed that led Arthur eventually to become a guard, a job he found sufficiently congenial to stick at for nearly thirty years.

'Well, it all came about by chance, I suppose. There was a big smash when a Bristol to London train left Swindon and the driver, who obviously thought he was on the main line, ran into the stop blocks on a loop. The train that crashed had been carrying a load of cigarettes and the shunters called in were told they could smoke the fags that lay about all over the place, but that they mustn't take them home with them. Inevitably some cigarettes were taken, and when one of the shunter's homes was raided the authorities found tons of other stolen gear. Nine shunters were sacked as a result of that incident, which meant the GWR at Swindon was suddenly very short of shunters. I applied for a transfer but because they couldn't get anyone to work in the foundry to replace me they wouldn't let me go. So I resigned and then reapplied for one of the shunter's jobs.'

Arthur became an under shunter and spent the next two years, as he describes it, running around like a two-year-old. But what did an under shunter do?

'Well, I'll take you through it. As the trains came in to Swindon the head shunter would look at the labels on the wagons and decide where they had to go. He'd pick up groups of wagons and send them off to different places. The under shunter pulled the points to make this happen. Then he used his shunting pole – 7ft long, made of wood and with a hook on the end – to couple the wagons together.

'This took some getting used to. Coal wagons, for example, were incredibly heavy and as they rolled towards each other you hooked your pole on to the coupling and slung it over. It took good timing to get it right and if you missed – which did happen – you had to run to the side of the wagon and put the handbrake on, otherwise it would hit the next wagon.

'We did mostly coal wagons, some wood and general freight of all kinds – we were always busy because very little freight went by road in those days. Apart from anything else there were no motorways, and Swindon was virtually in the centre of the southern part of the country. The amount of goods traffic going through was phenomenal.'

It took three years to go from being an under shunter to head shunter and the top rate of pay. Arthur, restless as ever, didn't want to wait that long and discovered that if he applied to become a guard his pay would immediately rise to a sum equivalent to that of a head shunter.

Special last train: a 2-6-0 4MT steam locomotive on its final run in December 1966

'I couldn't resist it,' he says, 'apart from the money I knew that a guard's job was a lot easier than a shunter's. The poor old shunter was on his feet all day with just a twenty-minute break between the third and fifth hours of his eight-hour shift. The freight guard's life was much less arduous once the train was out on the main line. You still had to do the shunting at the smaller yards where there was no permanent shunter and when you pulled off to pick up empty wagons. But when you were on your way you had time to sit back and think.'

When a guard came on duty the procedure was pretty much the same as for any other railwayman. He would book on by signing a sheet in the guard's room. Then he would either be given a specific job or he'd be what was called 'under control' – that is, available for any jobs that might come up during the shift.

'If I had a specific job to do, I'd first collect all my gear and then go to my train. The shunters would have formed the train already. They would then tell me which parts of the train had vacuum brakes. Freight was given a class: class 1 was coal, class 3 ordinary goods.

'You needed to know all this because you had to know how much the engine could pull and whether the whole train would fit in the shortest loop on your route. The driver drove the engine, remember, but the guard was in charge of the train.

'Anyway, I'd write down the tally of labels – there might be coal from South Wales destined for Horsham or Crawley, so different parts of the train had to be formed and then re-formed according to their different destinations. We had north of the Thames destinations in one section of the train and south of the Thames destinations in another – it was a complicated business.'

It was the guard's duty, once the train had been formed, to walk along its full length examining every wagon's brake, couplings and door pins. He'd then trim the lamps in the guard's van, light his little stove and check he had enough coal for the journey.

'I used to give the van a good clean out, too because that van was going to be my home for the next five or six hours – I wanted it to be as comfortable as possible!'

Having hooked the engine on, the guard would connect the vacuum and test the brakes. His next job was to tell the driver the load, the length of the train, the places it was due to stop to put on more wagons or take them off. Finally, as the driver started to pull away, the guard would walk back along the train to the van. Then he'd exchange hand signals with the fireman to prove the train was in one piece – these were procedures that probably hadn't changed in a century and they were strictly maintained because they worked. Like so many old railwaymen Arthur finds it difficult to understand how the modern railway can expect to be run safely and efficiently when it has discarded these and other working practices.

'The guard really was just that – a guard. It was his job to make sure the train was in running order before it left and to make sure it went where it was supposed to go safely and on time!'

The word 'guard', like the word 'coach', goes back to the days of horse-drawn transport. The early history of the railway also gave the signalman the nickname

'Bobby', for the early signalmen 'policed' the railway even to the extent of always having a truncheon in their boxes – hence the name which survived right up until the end of steam working.

A typical freight train might have only half a dozen wagons fitted with vacuum brakes. The rest would be loose-coupled. The guard who knew his job would keep in mind the number of vacuum-braked wagons and he would use his brake to keep all the other couplings tight to ensure as smooth a ride as possible. He had to know the road and the dips and rises. He would brake for the dips to prevent the wagons catching up on each other and take the brake off for the rises where gravity would keep the train tight. The control of the whole train was, in this sense, in the guard's hands.

'If you didn't use your brake as you went down hill all the loose-coupled wagons would bang into each other and you'd have a hell of a ride, or a coupling would brake and you'd have a divided train. Sometimes, however careful you were, this still happened and you'd then stop your bit of the train hoping that the driver up front would quickly realize that he'd lost some wagons. Once you'd brought your bit of the divided train to a halt you'd climb down on to the track and start walking back. At ¼ mile you'd put a detonator on the track. At ½ mile you'd put two detonators on the track, three at ¾ mile, and so on. You'd keep walking till you got to the last signal box, where you'd report what had happened. The front part of the train would in the meantime have stopped at the next signal box up ahead – assuming the driver had noticed something was wrong. If he hadn't, the next signalman would see there was no tail light on the train and he'd contact the next signalman so the signals could be changed to stop the train.'

For an incident like this meticulous records were kept. The guard would have to record everything. Once the front portion of the train had stopped he'd then have to walk to it, which could mean a 5-mile hike or more because there were no two-way radios or telephones in those days. Once he'd caught up with the driver the guard would hand over what was called the wrong line order. This would have been completed by the guard at the signal box behind the divided train. If the driver agreed with the details the guard would ride on the rear of the front portion of the train, waving the driver back to the stranded portion of the train. Guards always kept spare couplings so the wagons could be repaired. They also kept blocks of wood to ram between spokes in the case of a runaway wagon, as well as special shoes for re-railing a derailed wagon.

'We had a lot of gear,' says Arthur. 'We had to have twelve detonators – little circular discs that would explode when a train went over them – oil lamps, a red flag and a green one, and spare oil for the lamp. The other strange thing is that the railway would never trust a driver to have a watch – only the guard was issued with one. The guard also kept a journal and at the end of each shift he'd fill it in: there were little boxes for each signal and how much time you spent waiting both there and while shunting and at stations. If you were late you had to write a report explaining why.

'If a train was due to leave at 2am you'd book on at 1.30am. If you were on a control link where you booked on and worked under a controller – that is, you had no specific job – you might end up sitting in the cabin by the fire for eight hours and then go home without doing a single thing. This sounds a bit wasteful, but it made sense because there was always a back-up crew if there was a problem. Today they wouldn't do it because they're obsessed with cutting costs.'

Railwaymen always talk about their great camaraderie, but it is easy to forget that this existed only between men in the same job. Drivers and firemen might mix with each other, but not with guards. Signalmen mixed only with other signalmen if they mixed at all; they were famously loners. Arthur remembers a bit of doggerel verse which neatly sums up the relationship between drivers and guards:

The guard is the man
Who rides in the van
The van at the rear of the train
The driver up front
Thinks the guard's a fool
And the guard thinks the driver's the same.

'I'm afraid it's not a joke,' says Arthur with an amused grin and wry shake of the head. 'Guards never went into the engine room, and drivers never went into the guards' room. But then, as I've said, it was all a matter of respect and formality – the railways were run on very strict lines. You wouldn't cross the floor of the signal box without asking permission – you didn't dare – but if that was the down side of the old system it also had huge benefits. The old rule book, for example, was designed in such a way that everyone covered everyone else. If one man made a mistake another man would very likely pick it up.'

But life was spartan too at that time. There were no canteens for guards or drivers, and in the guards' room management would have thought it very bad for morale to provide comfortable chairs.

Double-headed: a 3MT 2-6-2T in front, with a 4MT 2-6-0 behind, February 1966

'We just had bare wooden benches because it wasn't the idea to make you comfortable in the company's time. We got round the problem by bringing in our own chairs – some men brought in big old armchairs, or they'd get an old leather seat that had been used on the platform or in one of the passenger waiting rooms.'

Arthur worked trains down to Bristol, Cardiff, Exeter, Banbury and Old Oak Common in West London. The area covered by the GWR was so great, and its reputation so impressive, that GWR men could get credit almost anywhere.

'My father could get credit in London in the days when a Swindon bricklayer couldn't get it in the shop at the corner of his street,' says Arthur. 'And in Swindon you didn't ask a man what he did for a living – you asked him, "Are you in or out?" Everyone knew that meant, "Do you work for the Great Western Railway or for someone else?"'

When steam began to disappear there were huge problems, not just for drivers and firemen but also for guards. Drivers didn't appreciate at first the huge difference between the new engines and the old. Many guards ended up in hospital as the new diesel engines were more powerful and so accelerated far more quickly than steam engines. Arthur again. 'With diesel, as you set off, the wagons were much more likely to snatch and the train would start to lurch about. The poor old guard then got thrown around unless he was well wedged in – so that's what we started to do.'

But apart from that, for a number of years after steam disappeared the guard's life was pretty much the same. 'It was still the same old bloody van!' says Arthur. But the design of the van differed between regions.

'The GWR guard's van had a veranda at one end. Midland region vans had a veranda at both ends. The brake itself – an old-fashioned thing that you literally screwed down by turning a handle round and round – was slap bang in the middle of the van. We had what we called a bubble on either side of the van, basically a small window. According to the rule book you were supposed to remain alert and vigilant at all times, but once diesel came in we used to say that you were safer lying down on the floor with the guard's bag under your head. In the bag we'd have all our gear, as well as tea, milk and sugar and something to eat – and of course you had your little stove so you could heat things up. It was easier doing it this way than frying your eggs on the shovel, which is what I used to do when I was firing.

'Guards were always famous for having classy newspapers like *The Times* and the *Observer* – they didn't read them, but they were ideal for folding into strips to keep the draughts out of the van!

'In summer of course the guard's van was a far more attractive proposition. We used to open the doors on to the veranda and sit out there. It turned me into a Walter Mitty character, a daydreamer, particularly in winter because you spent hours in the near dark with no light to read – the old oil lamp didn't throw out enough light to see a book or a newspaper.'

Arthur worked as a Great Western guard for twenty-eight years. He would have continued until retirement, but a heart attack put paid to that and he spent his last

Credit: National Railway Museum/Science & Society

HIKE for HEALTH
SOUTHERN RAILWAY
Go-as-you-please cheap tickets
get you to the country quickest

Ask for details at any S·R Office and buy
"Southern Rambles" by S·P·B·Mais 6D

years on light duties – mostly collecting tickets at the barrier. When he retired due to ill health he'd completed nearly forty-three years' service. But what were the highlights?

'Well, we all thought that becoming British Rail in 1948 would be a big change, but it wasn't. They just changed the colour of the engines. Another highlight – well, more a lowlight really – was when I had a burst hotbox just outside the Chipping Sodbury tunnel. The hotbox was a box filled with oil that kept the axles lubricated. They'd replaced the old grease boxes, but the pads of material in them that held the oil were supposed to be soaked for twenty-four hours before being fitted. If someone in the works rushed the job and there was not enough oil the axle rubbed on the bearing – in other words metal on metal – and you had a big problem. The box would catch fire and the axle would then collapse. I knew a fair bit about this from my days cutting up old wagons and salvaging bits of them.

'Anyway, the hotbox collapsed and the wagon that went over tore up about 5 miles of track. I was thrown around but wasn't badly hurt. I suspect the box wouldn't have gone only the driver was going too fast, but he got away with it.'

The old system of oiling axles has long vanished. It outlasted steam itself but not by much. The old-style guard and his van are also long gone, along with the extraordinary institutions and structure of the old Great Western. As well as running its own buses and coal mines and making every conceivable item necessary for railway work, the Great Western ran tests on everything, even down to the wood used to make the coaches.

'If you looked out of the carriage window on one stretch of track near Wantage you used to see lots of wood panels on a hoarding – they were all left there, completely open to the elements, to test their durability. It was the perfect spot because not only did they have to put up with the weather, they also had all the steam and smuts from passing trains.'

The boy who failed his first railway test before the war didn't quite give up his connection with the railway after retirement. Arthur still sees other railwaymen regularly, and after a short time as a local councillor he became mayor of Swindon, and no ordinary mayor at that: he was the last railway mayor who once worked for the old Great Western Railway.

'Well, over half of Swindon's mayors were railwaymen, but only the very old like me can still remember the days before British Rail when the Great Western Railway was always known among the men by its nickname: God's Wonderful Railway. Gone With Regret.'

Engine trouble

The *Edinburgh Chronicle* must take the responsibility of vouching the truth of the story that follows: 'A gentleman, on urgent business in Glasgow, arrived at the Edinburgh station on Monday morning just as the 9 o'clock train had started. A special engine was engaged, and, starting at half past 9 o'clock, overtook the train at Falkirk at 10 minutes past 10 o'clock, running the 23 miles in 40 minutes, 15 minutes of which time was occupied in stopping at three of the stations; the 23 miles were thus traversed in 25 minutes, being at the enormous speed of 55 miles in an hour.' More remarkable yet is the statement of a correspondent of the *Railway Times,* who gives his name and address as 'George Wall, Sheffield, 7th December, 1843':

'I have frequently timed trains to 60 to 65 seconds to the mile, and on one occasion a train ran 3 miles in 53, 54, and 55 seconds respectively, giving an average of 54 seconds per mile, or 59½ miles per hour. In this last case two other passengers marked the time, along with me, by our own watches, and we were all agreed.'

This perhaps helps us to understand why trains, which could travel on occasion as fast as this, were not timed faster in everyday working, to read that among the indispensable appliances on a railway were included trucks on which to convey broken-down engines, and also a suggestion that a trolley should always be attached in front of the engine, that it might be ready at hand to fetch assistance in case of a breakdown.
The Railways of England, W. M. Acworth, 1889

Horse dung in the boiler

There was a practice – described as almost universal before the recent improvements in engine building – of putting oatmeal of bran or, if these could not be had, horse dung into the boiler in order to stop the leaking of the tubes.
The History of the English Railway, J. Francis, 1851

Record specials

It was looked on as a remarkable feat that Mr Allport travelled from Sunderland to London and back with relays of specials in waiting at Darlington, York, Normanton, Derby, Rugby and Wolverton – 600 miles in 15 hours.

Not only were the engines too small to run more than 20 or 30 miles without taking in water, but there were numerous spots where the permanent way was not wholly to be trusted. Here it had shown a tendency to subside, there the sides of a cutting looked like slipping.
The History of the English Railway, J. Francis, 1851

Suspicious tunnel

Dean Buckland was not alone in suspecting the Box Tunnel. The public mind was so uneasy on the subject, that General Pasley was sent down by the Board of Trade to make a special inspection. He reported it sound and safe, and added 'that the concussion of air from the passage of the locomotive was not likely to endanger the safety of passengers' by bringing down the roof where the tunnel was cut through the live rock without the arch being bricked. No doubt the mere fact that it was a tunnel was enough to make many people suspect it. In January 1842 the *Glasgow Argus* reported, in reference to the Cowlairs Tunnel on the Edinburgh and Glasgow, that 'as the lamps, 43 in number, will be kept burning night and day during the passage of the various trains, the, dull, cheerless and to many alarming, feelings which passing through a dark tunnel usually excites, will be entirely removed, the effect being little else than the passage through a, somewhat, narrow street. The tunnel presents a very splendid appearance, while it creates a feeling of the utmost security, although the spectator is conscious of the immense super-incumbent masses of rock and other strata which are resting above him.'

A year or two earlier it needed more than mere gaslights to reassure the British public. 'The deafening peal of thunder,' said one medical authority, 'the sudden immersion in gloom, and the clash of reverberated sounds in a confined space, combine to produce a momentary shudder or idea of destruction, a thrill of annihilation.'
The Railways of England, W. M. Acworth, 1889

Caution needed

The truth seems to be that accidents were frequent rather than serious. Neither the companies' servants nor the public had learned to treat railway trains with the necessary caution. Engine drivers fancied that collision between two engines was much the same thing as the interlocking of the wheels of two rival stage coaches.
The History of the English Railway, J. Francis, 1851

Going too fast

The Prince Consort, too, was not the only person who protested against over-rapid travelling. The newspapers are full of complaints of dangerous speed. One correspondent suggests that notice boards shall be fixed all along the line, prescribing the due speed for each stretch lest the engine-driver should be tempted to exceed the bounds of prudence. Another proposed to forbid all speed in excess of 20 miles an hour exclusive of stoppages, and 'to ensure this not being exceeded there should be a method adopted by which the engine would give notice of the same to every passenger, that they might report upon it.

'I am prepared to produce a plan by which this can be effected. The whistle might be blown (ie, utter a slight sound) at every $\frac{1}{4}$ or $\frac{1}{2}$ mile, being worked by the driving wheel.

'And this arrangement would be attended with another advantage, viz, in a fog. It might then sound to its full power giving not only notice of its approach, but some idea of the speed; and, if generally understood that the whistle of the down train sounded six seconds, whilst that of the up train uttered its note only three, there would be no mistake as to which train was approaching.'
Railway Appliances, J. W. Barry, 1884

Tunnel testing

Here is what Lieutenant Le Count found it necessary to publish as to the London and Birmingham: 'So much has been said about the inconvenience and danger of tunnels, that it is necessary whilst there are yet so

many railways to be called into existence, to state that there is positively no inconvenience whatever in them, except the change from daylight to lamplight. This matter was clearly investigated and proved on the London and Birmingham Railway, a special inspection having been there made in the Primrose Hill tunnel by Dr Paris and Dr Watson, Messrs Lawrence and Lucas, surveyors, and Mr Phillips, lecturer on chemistry, who reported as follows:

'We, the undersigned, visited together, on the 20th of February, 1837, the tunnel now in progress under Primrose Hill, with the view of ascertaining the probable effect of such tunnels upon the health and feeling, of those who may traverse them.

The First Passenger Coach

'The tunnel is carried through clay, and is laid with brickwork. Its dimensions as described to us, are as follows: height, 22ft; length 3,750ft; width, 22ft. It is ventilated by five shafts from 6ft to 8ft in diameter, the depth being 35 to 55ft.

'The experiment was made under unfavourable circumstances; the western extremity being only partially open, ventilation is less perfect than it will be when the work is completed; the steam of the locomotive engine was also offered to escape for twenty minutes, while the carriages were stationary, near the end of the tunnel; even during our stay near the unfinished end of the tunnel, where the engine remained stationary, although the cloud caused by the steam was visible near the roof, the air for many feet above our heads remained clear and apparently uninfected by steam or effluvia of any kind, neither was there any damp or cold perceptible. We found the atmosphere of the tunnel dry and of an agreeable temperature, and free from smell.

'The carriages were lighted, and in our transit inwards and back again to the mouth of the tunnel the sensation experienced was precisely that of travelling in a coach by night between the walls of a narrow street. The noise did not prevent easy conversation, nor appear to be much greater in the tunnel than in the open air. Judging from this experiment, and knowing the ease and certainty with which through ventilation may be effected, we are decidedly of opinion that the dangers incurred in passing through well- constructed tunnels are no greater than those incurred in ordinary travelling upon an open railway or upon a turnpike road, and that the apprehensions which have been expressed that such tunnels are likely to prove detrimental to the health, or inconvenient, the feelings of those who may go through them, are perfectly futile and groundless.'

The Railways of England, W. M. Acworth, 1889

Drunk in charge

Accidents were naturally of frequent occurrence, taking mainly the shape of collisions. Here, for example, is a record for a single line, the North Midland, for a single week of January 1843, as given by a correspondent of the *Railway Times* of that date. This company appears to have engaged several new drivers, one of whom had just been released from Wakefield Gaol, where he had served two months' imprisonment for being 'in a beastly state of intoxication' when in charge of an engine.

Jan 2: No. 48 engine, sent out to bring in a broken horse-box; connecting rod broke, and that broke the cylinder cover, and otherwise seriously damaged the working gear.

Jan 3: Before the goods train out of Leeds at 8pm arrived at Masbro – a distance of thirty-two miles – the driver was compelled to draw his fire out. He afterwards arrived at Derby six hours late. (This engineman only worked a stationary engine before.) The eight o'clock into Derby overtook a coal train about three miles from Derby with four engines attached to it, the gatekeeper informing the alarmed and trembling passengers that it was only a coal train that had obstructed the line for five hours. The cause of employing so many engines was that three of them were sent out as pilots, one after the other, but unfortunately got so disabled themselves that they were unable to render the necessary assistance.

Jan 5: No. 11 engine running the mail train out of Derby broke down after running eight miles. It cannot be put into a proper state of repair for months. No. 9 engine damaged very much in the firebox. The 10.15 train into Derby broke down.

Jan 6: The 3.15 out of Derby broke down. The 5.30pm passenger train from Leeds was standing at Barnsley Station when the driver of a luggage train ran into it. There was fortunately only one passenger. The carriages were all smashed to pieces and the head of the unfortunate passenger was cut completely off.
Railway Reminiscences, G. P. Neele, 1904

Locomotive sails

This very year, 1843, a paper read before the Society of Arts advocated the adoption of a continuous steam-brake. In 'the absence of efficient brakes, one railway in America is reported to be using sails to check the velocity of trains on steep inclines'.
The History of the English Railway, J. Francis, 1851

Going third class

Third-class trains from London to Taunton took sixteen hours over the 163 miles, leaving London either at 9pm or 4am. When a shareholder pleaded for greater speed, he was met by the 'answer that passengers in third-class carriages would not be able to endure the exposure to the weather if they travelled more rapidly'. To Liverpool and Manchester there was one third-class train only in the twenty-four hours, and passengers had to wait at Birmingham from 3pm till 6 o'clock next morning.

Many lines, the Liverpool and Manchester, and the Newcastle and Carlisle, for instance, at this time carried no third-class passengers at all.

It should be said also that, on local lines in manufacturing districts, eg, between Sheffield and Rotherham, Leeds and Manchester, or North Shields and Newcastle, quite a different state of things prevailed. Third-class passengers were not only booked by all trains, but, in one instance at least, were conveyed in covered carriages, furnished with seats. The consequence was that the Newcastle and North Shields line carried in the first months of 1841 seven times as many third-class passengers as travelled over the whole system of the London and Birmingham and the Grand Junction put together.

Railway Reminiscences, G. P. Neele, 1904

Mountain climber

'Want of faith in the capabilities of the locomotive engine has formed one important item in the cost of the English railway system. Engineers set out in their railway career with the impression that the locomotive was ill calculated to climb uphill with its load, and that therefore, to work with advantage, it must work on lines altogether level, or nearly

so; hence mountains required to be levelled, valleys filled up, tunnels pierced through rocks; and viaducts reared in the air, gigantic works at a gigantic cost, all for the purpose of enabling the engine to travel along a dead level, or nearly so. But here, again, was want of faith in the power of the locomotive engine. The locomotive engine can climb the mountain-side as well as career along the plain.' So wrote the *Athenaeum* in 1843, and so, in fact, it was proved in the next few years, when the Lancaster and Carlisle was carried over Shap Fell at a height of 915ft above the sea, with a gradient of 1 in 75 for 4 miles, and the Caledonian climbed for 10 miles at a gradient of 1 in 80 to Beattock Summit, 1,015ft above sea level.

The Railways of England, W. M. Acworth, 1889

Left behind

Here is a story from the 1840s from the *Globe:* 'A gentleman persisted, though advised to the contrary, in riding in his own carriage on the train to Brighton. In the Balcombe tunnel, the truck on which the gentleman's carriage was fastened, which was the last vehicle, became disengaged. The unfortunate occupant, perceiving the train leaving him, called after them, but in vain; and, finding they proceeded on their journey, he became dreadfully alarmed, being afraid to alight, and not knowing whether in a few minutes he might not be dashed to pieces by the next train. He had not been long in this suspense when an engine entered the tunnel, puffing away and the whistle screaming. He now considered his doom sealed; but the engine proved to be a pilot one sent to look after him, the truck and carriage having fortunately been missed on the train's arrival at the next station. The carriage and occupant were then conveyed to Brighton, where they arrived soon after

the train, and the only damage was the great fright the gentleman sustained.'

Of a different class was an accident at Tewkesbury: 'At the top end of the station was a gateway, and beyond this a line of rails which crosses the public street and leads down to the river Severn. There was some scaffolding erected inside the gateway, which would admit of an engine to pass under it; but on this occasion the engine proceeded at full speed through the gateway and the scaffolding catching the chimney, down it came, crushing the gateway, and the engine getting into the street, a pig that was passing at the time was run over and killed on the spot.'
Railway Reminiscences, G. P. Neele, 1904

Seafaring guards

It should be added that, in addition to the driver and fireman, it had been proposed to have a third man on the engine, who should be supplied with a small telescope in order that he might keep a good look-out ahead; of course, the protection of a cab had not yet been thought of, and the men were as entirely unprotected from the weather as though they were driving, not an engine, but an old stage coach.

So too were the guards, who sat on the top of the train, the head guard on the last carriage facing forward, the under-guard on the front carriage looking back to see that his train was duly following – a thing which it must be confessed some portion at least of the train not unfrequently failed to do.

The luggage was commonly placed on the top beside them, and down to a much later period than this (the 1840s) there were eleven strappers at Euston whose special function it was to keep the straps which fastened the luggage duly greased, lest, becoming brittle, they break and the luggage roll off on the journey. The guards, said

Lieutenant Le Count, should be furnished with wire spectacles to protect their eyes from the ashes constantly thrown out of the engine chimney till some means are found of remedying this unpleasant defect. They, the guards, should by preference be old seamen, as they will be found accustomed to lashings.
The History of the English Railway, J. Francis, 1851

Rope driven

The London & Blackwall Railway was worked by stationary engines, dragging the carriages with one wire rope for the up and another for the down traffic, each having a total length of about 8 miles and a weight of 40 tons. And on this line, among the first, the electric telegraph was used, in order that the

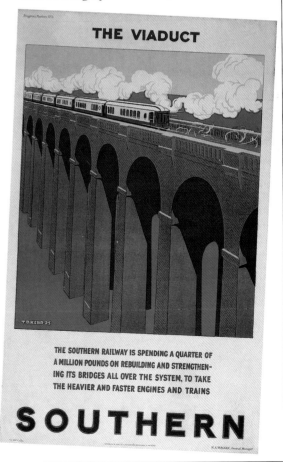

THE VIADUCT

THE SOUTHERN RAILWAY IS SPENDING A QUARTER OF A MILLION POUNDS ON REBUILDING AND STRENGTHENING ITS BRIDGES ALL OVER THE SYSTEM, TO TAKE THE HEAVIER AND FASTER ENGINES AND TRAINS

SOUTHERN

Credit: National Railway Museum/Science & Society

engineer at Blackwall or Fenchurch Street might know when to begin to wind up or let go his rope.

The system in use was certainly most ingenious. A down train, as it left Fenchurch Street, consisted of seven carriages. The two in front went through to Blackwall; the next carriage only as far as Poplar, and so on to the seventh, which was detached at Shadwell, the first station after leaving Fenchurch Street. As the train approached Shadwell, the guard, standing on a platform in front of the carriage, pulled out 'a pin from the coupling at an interval of time sufficient to let the carriage arrive at its proper destination by the momentum acquired in its passage from London'.

The same process was repeated at each subsequent station, till finally the two remaining carriages ran up the terminal incline, and were brought to a stand at the Blackwall station. On the return journey the carriage at each station was attached to the rope at a fixed hour, and then the whole series were set in motion simultaneously, so that they arrived at Fenchurch Street at, 'intervals proportioned to the distance between the stations'. But the

wear and tear was too much; there were perpetual delays owing to the rope breaking and the cost of repairs and renewals was something immense.

The Sunderland and Durham also was worked with a rope, at first of hemp and afterwards of wire, as was and still is the Cowlairs tunnel on the Edinburgh and Glasgow line. On other similar local lines, such as the Edinburgh and Dalkeith, or the Dundee and Arbroath, the carriages were still drawn by horses.

In Ireland, again, the continuation of the Dublin and Kingstown Railway on to Dalkey, which was worked by atmospheric engines, was just being opened for traffic, a speed of about 30 miles an hour having been successfully obtained on several trial trips, it was proposed to work the line from Exeter to Plymouth by water power. Water power, however, was abandoned, and the atmospheric system adopted, and this was so far at least a success, that on one occasion the 8 miles between Exeter and Starcross were said to have been covered at the rate of 70 miles an hour.

The Railways of England, W. M. Acworth, 1889

FIFTY YEARS ON THE FOOT PLATE

Mick Leslie,
Fireman and driver

I was a tailboard monkey before I became a railwayman,' Mick Leslie announces, before explaining that he can't say much about the dodges he used to get up in those far-off days during the war. 'My mates would never forgive me,' he continues with a huge grin. 'Mind you, most of them are dead now – just a few of us still hanging on.'

But just what *is* a tailboard monkey?

'It's the van boy, the lad who sits on the back of a delivery van and jumps off every time something has to be taken off.' But when Mick started work he was the van boy on a horse and cart. 'Yeah, I was probably one of the last to do that sort of work.'

From horse and cart Mick moved to Scammel lorries. 'I got 16/- [80p] a week and I bet not many people remember the Scammels now – they had three wheels instead of four. You don't see many of those around! We went all over the place but London was completely different then – no skyscrapers, all narrow lanes and smoke-blackened houses from the coal fires.'

Mick already knew the capital well as he'd been born in Hackney in 1925 and brought up in Southgate. He left school at fourteen. Today he lives in the little semi-detached house he bought over forty years ago in Potters Bar on the hills just beyond where North London ends and Hertfordshire begins.

In 1941 Mick decided to try for a job on the railways.

'I had friends in the loco depot. They told me it wasn't bad so I applied, had my interview and was given 30/- [£1.50p] a week to clean engines at King's Cross top shed 34A. We did all the usual filthy work – right under the engine, pistons, side rods, the lot. But the youngest cleaners had to do the fire lighting too. That was a hard job – no sixteen-year-old now would even think of doing it. He probably wouldn't be allowed to. There was a big place where we would collect shovelfuls of red-hot coal and we had to carry these across to whichever engine had to be lit.'

After eighteen months' cleaning Mick began to assist the shunters in top shed 34A. He would set the points for the engines to go in and out of the shed.

'We had all sorts then – Atlantics, A4s, Pacifics, N2s, J52s – but at that stage all you knew about them was that they had to be cleaned!'

Mick has very happy memories of his early cleaning days. He was with other lads roughly the same age and with similar interests; lads who always had time for fun and practical jokes.

'We had a great time. When the foreman wasn't around we chucked the swabs at each other and then had to run and hide if we saw him coming. I was never bored – that's why I stayed so long.'

But the shed work never stopped, day and night. Running continually on three eight-hour shifts (the men started at either 6am, 2pm or 10pm), the shed was a scene of never-ending noise, smoke and fire.

'It was always busy, yes, but very well organized because you were kept an eye on by the different foremen – some of them were right bastards, but others were really good.'

Mick took the train each day to King's Cross from his home, which at that time was at Southgate in North London. After two years of cleaning and point setting in the sheds he was passed as a cleaner. It was 1943 and the war was raging; the goods yard at King's Cross was busier than ever, and it was here that Mick started firing.

'I worked on J52s, shunting engines. I thought it was really funny because a lot of the old boys would fall asleep on the footplate and let you do all the firing and driving for them. But it took me ten years as a fireman to be passed for driving. I was thirty by this time – it would have been 1956 – and I remember one old driver, who started driving just after World War I ended, still saying to me, "I don't know what the railways are coming to now we've got boys like you driving". In a way he was right, because but for the war it probably would have taken a lot longer to become a driver. The war and the effect it had afterwards because of the shortage of men accelerated everything.'

As a fireman and then driver Mick gradually moved up the links. He started in the Metropolitan gang doing local services, then moved to No. 4 gang driving main-line trains to Peterborough. No. 3 gang saw him taking trains to Doncaster. No. 2 meant Leeds, and finally No. 1 gang drove the passenger train to Newcastle and the non-stop to Edinburgh.

'On the Metropolitan link I used to fire a lot for a bloke called Arthur Howe. He was great because we used to swap the work about – I'd fire one day and then he'd fire the next, which meant I got a lot of driving experience. On the Edinburgh non-stop top passenger link you'd be firing almost continually, but only as far as York where what we called the "Jock crew" would take over. They were Edinburgh Haymarket men. We'd walk back through the tender to our own washroom – "washroom" meant a bucket of water on the floor! And the Jock crew would take over the train – that way we didn't have to stop. There was a narrow passageway back through the tender and what we called the washroom was actually a separate compartment, where we could clean up and get changed. Once or twice we went back only to find that a passenger was in there. I found a couple there once and even though I explained that it was for footplate men only they refused to move. I didn't know what to do for a minute. Then I had an idea. I said to them, "Well, if you're going to stay, I'm afraid I'm still going to get changed", and that involved taking all my clothes off. As soon as I started to strip they were off like a shot!

'Once we'd washed as well as we could – not easy in a bucket – we'd go down the train to the buffet car and have a drink or two with the passengers. Sometimes they'd come up to the footplate and we'd make a few bob that way because they'd give us a tip for letting them see how we did things. It wasn't really allowed, but my boss used to say, "I just don't want to know".'

Like so many old railwaymen Mick remembers much of the railwayman's slang, a whole host of words and phrases peculiar to the industry. "Bent dart" referred to the heavy poker used for cleaning clinker from the firebox; "boomerang" was a return ticket; "bobby" was a signalman (because the signalman was like a policeman) and "bug dust" was the name given to very small pieces of coal.

Mick also remembers the extraordinary number of drivers and firemen with nicknames. Almost every man was known by some name not his own, but, as Mick explains, he never had one.

'I don't know why that was – maybe Mick was short and sweet enough on its own! We had some right funny nicknames for other men, though – I can remember Banana Jim, Peanut Jo and Burglar Allan. Funny thing is, you knew their nicknames but almost never how they got them.'

In 1948 Mick met his future wife. She was a guard on the Metropolitan link at the time they met. A friend of Mick's bet him that he wouldn't have the courage to ask her for a date.

'He said, "Go on – I'll give you a dollar if you do". Well, not only did I ask her out – I married her. And you know what – I never did get my dollar!'

Mick is convinced that one of the main reasons enginemen so rarely left to seek other work was that they were always learning. The job was never dull. At each stage in the promotion-by-seniority process there was something new to get to grips with. Of course there were also the fascinating characters, older men who'd come up through the ranks during and just after World War I.

'Yes, there were some real characters. I remember one old boy I fired for – Harold Hutchins Panshine was his name – Panshine on account of his permanent red, shiny face. In all the time I fired for him I don't think I ever saw old Panshine without a swab in his hand. He'd stand on that footplate continually wiping and polishing the brass pipes. He was like a driver who couldn't bear the fact that he was no longer a cleaner! One day I told him I'd help him clean the floor, but only if I could tie rags around my feet and use them!'

Mick also fired for Bill Waddingham who'd started work after World War I. Bill wore a bib-and-brace and a great heavy overall coat.

'That coat was like a bloody coal sack,' recalls Mick. 'It was so big and black and dirty it made him look like a piece of coal!'

Mick refuses to adopt an entirely nostalgic view of his early working days, but his realism is tempered by a wry humour and a great capacity for enjoying even difficult situations.

'Don't let anyone tell you that engine driving in winter was comfortable because you had a firebox to keep you warm: it wasn't. It was bloody freezing a lot of the time. And on the top links where we drove to Leeds, say, our lodgings were bloody awful, too! At Newcastle they were even worse. I can remember sometimes I had to wait for someone else to get out of bed before I could get in!'

Mick has a wealth of memories about the odd quirky corners of railway life – such as the fish train he fired on a number of times. It was no ordinary fish train, but the one that brought cod, haddock and sole from the East Coast to London specifically for Buckingham Palace. Mick also recalls the wooden name tablets on the wall in the mess room at King's Cross.

'They had all the men's names on and were shuffled about according to where you were working, but someone must have got a bit over-enthusiastic with the drivers' fire we all used to crowd round because the tablets were all burnt at one end.

'We used to play terrible tricks on anyone sleeping in the mess room, too. It was always warm with that big fire going day and night so the old men would get round the zinc table and fall asleep. We'd then get an old sack over the fire till the room was filled with smoke. They'd wake up in a rage!'

But whatever else happened on the railways, when a man came in for his shift something was always found for him to do.

'When you were pretty junior it could be anything – preparing an engine, or later

on driving god knows where. And some turns were awful – the worst was the 3am start because to be there at that time you had to catch the last train the night before, which got you there three or four hours before you were needed, and the company didn't pay you for that time. And once you were there all you could do was sit about and wait. I often left home at 11pm and didn't get home till 2pm the next afternoon.'

In 1959, just as talk of the end of steam had begun, Mick was made a regular driver at £9 a week. Money and conditions generally were beginning to improve and, with the advent of the new trains, life on the railways in some ways suddenly felt better.

'Diesels were so clean and easy to drive after steam. On the footplate when you were firing it often felt as if your arse was alight. Some men would put thick packing material all down their left sides to protect them from the intense heat every time they opened the firebox. On the non-stop trains it was non-stop for the fireman too – if you weren't shovelling coal into the firehole you were pulling it forward from the tender on to the shovelling plate – imagine doing that hour after hour without stopping. Then suddenly with the diesels – although they didn't come into full force until 1962 – it was all over.'

But although clean, easy driving had its advantages, some of the spark went out of the railways. Like most men at the time Mick welcomed the change since life became easier, but he knew too that the glory days were over.

'Well, we couldn't make the same jokes for a start,' says Mick with a smile. 'I remember I was climbing over the coal on the tender once – I was absolutely black from head to foot – and my driver Bill Andrews shouted up, "You look perfect now to go and collect the tickets from first class!"'

A Class K3 2-6-0 locomotive with a train of cattle vans in the early morning mist, circa 1950
Credit: National Railway Museum/Science & Society

Mick recalls the amazement he and his colleagues felt when they discovered that on American trains there was an automatic shoveller, where the fireman pressed a button and the coal was fed down to his position on the footplate.

'We had to do it with our bloody hands,' says Mick ruefully. But if the work was hard, there were many compensations, such as a terrific pride in their work, and the enjoyable friendly rivalry between drivers.

'We used to see who could go furthest without shutting off the regulator – that was all down to skill. Being the best driver, or at least a driver who never did anything really silly, was also a matter of pride. If you made a serious mistake it could stay with you for years. I remember one bloke driving his engine into the shed who got in a terrible mess; the water in his cylinders pushed back and bent the side rods on his engine. For years after that he was known as Side Rod Sid.'

When diesels came in Mick first drove what was called a Birmingham Carriage and Wagon; these were followed by Brushes and then Deltics, each type more powerful and reliable than its predecessor.

'The early diesels weren't a patch on steam when it came to power and they were very unreliable, but I worked on those and all the later models right up until I retired. When I finished I was the top driver in No. 1 gang at King's Cross, but by that time there were only one or two old boys like me who had any experience at all of the steam days. Now, of course, we're all retired or dead.'

Other memories crowd together as Mick explains how one day during the war he stood and watched a doodlebug approaching him at 3am. It was only when its

Courtesy of Milepost 92½ Picture Library

flame went out that he shook himself out of his reverie and headed for cover. Fortunately for him it flew on and exploded some miles away. He also remembers how, as a fireman, he would earn a bit more money by volunteering for fire-damping duties.

'We used to go round chucking water on the fires as they were thrown out of the engines that had finished for the day. It was horrible work but we were paid the labouring rate to do it, which was more than our usual rate. As a general rule, too, it was murder to get anything out of our bosses – they would do anything to save a ha'penny.'

When he finally retired Mick had experienced a fraction over fifty years on the railways, a remarkable record.

'It's funny, during all those years one of the things I remember best – apart from the lifelong friends I made – was driving the *Flying Scotsman* with Miss England and Miss Scotland aboard! That was a red-letter day because I got interviewed with them by the BBC! But I was quite happy to retire in the end. I knew I'd stay in touch with all my old mates while they were still alive and I think after fifty years I'd more or less done my bit. And at the end I was still walking for nearly an hour each morning to catch the train to work – it was about 3 miles. I'd certainly had enough of that!

'Railway life was hard, then, but I miss it even now.'

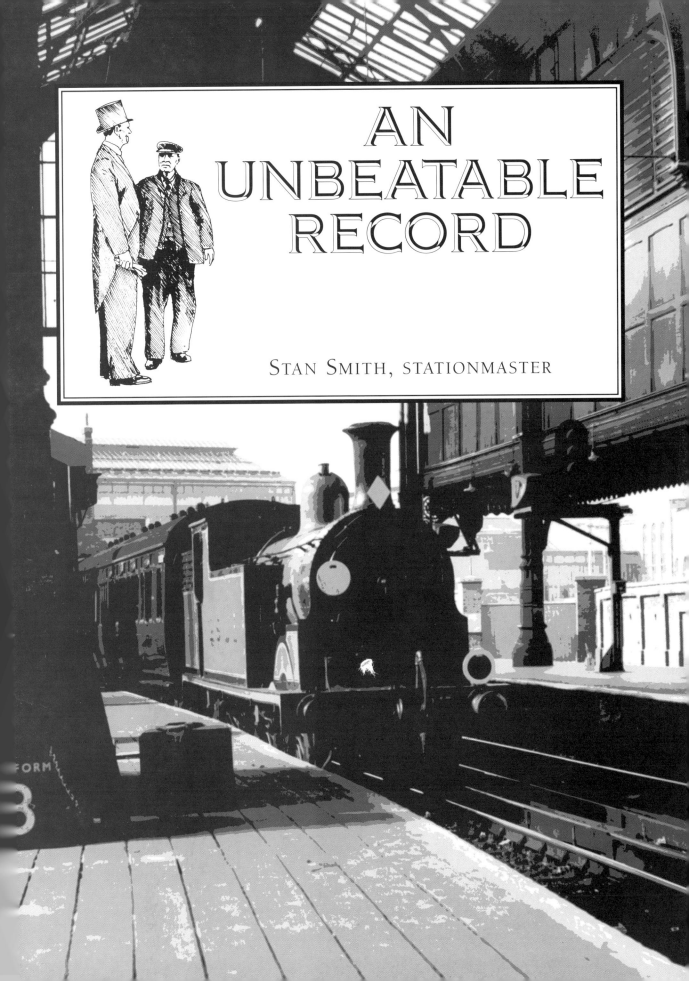

AN UNBEATABLE RECORD

Stan Smith, stationmaster

No one will ever now match the extraordinary record held by Sussex railwayman Stan Smith, for he is the fifth and last in a line of stationmasters, father and son, going back to 1840. With the job of stationmaster now long gone, Stan's family record can never be beaten.

He was born in 1921, and although as a schoolboy he dreamed occasionally of other careers, such notions were swept aside by his father who insisted he carry on the family tradition.

'It must have been hard for my dad, because he was very proud of being a stationmaster from a long line of stationmasters. He knew all about the family tradition and didn't want me to be the one to change it all. He also knew that a railway job was secure and for life. Before the war and during the Depression of the 1930s, when jobs were very difficult to find, the railway still needed a lot of men, but they tended to give railway jobs to railwaymen's sons. Might seem unfair now, but that was often the way things were done in those days and no one thought anything of it.'

But what of that extraordinary lineage? It all began with William Smith, Stan's great-great-grandfather. He joined the old London & Croydon Railway, the forerunner of the London, Brighton & South Coast Railway, in 1840. He became stationmaster at Anerley in what is now South London, and worked there from 1857 until he retired in 1878.

William's son, William Henry, worked for the same railway company and was stationmaster at Old Kent Road and then at Forest Hill, both stations in South London. After William Henry came Stan's grandfather, Alfred, who combined the job of stationmaster and postmaster at Amberley in Sussex. Stan's father Archie was a relief stationmaster on the Brighton line, opened the old Gatwick station, and retired as stationmaster at Chatham & Gillingham, Kent, in 1952.

Stan was born at Patcham on the edge of Brighton in Sussex, just a few miles from Seaford where he now lives comfortably in retirement with his wife Yvonne. He started work in 1938, and has never regretted that he stayed with the railways for the whole of his working life.

'Not a bit. I enjoyed it. Railwaymen are a great bunch and pretty much every day of my forty-two-year service was interesting – so it wasn't just the family tradition that kept me at it!'

Stan's first job was as a junior clerk at Burgess Hill station just a few miles up the line towards London from his home at Patcham.

'I used to cycle there every day and we did six days a week and shift work, either

seven until two or two till ten. You alternated between shifts: one week on the late shift, then a week on the early shift. Despite a long week by modern standards – forty-eight hours not including travel – I enjoyed the work. Even small country stations were very busy in those days, so you didn't have time to worry about how long the hours were or how interesting or otherwise the job was. You just had to get on with it. Most people forget just how much traffic went by rail then – tons of parcels, all the mail and all the newspapers – not to mention the passengers.

'Of course, being the junior clerk you were the lowest of the low – I did the accounts for the station, sold the tickets, worked out the pay for the station staff, made sure the parcels went on the right train and were loaded on to the railway cart. But they were innocent days too, because the stationmaster used to carry the station takings down to the local bank each week and collect the men's wages, and I don't

Stan's great-great-grandfather, William. He joined the London & Croydon Railway in 1840

think anyone thought for a moment it might be dangerous and he might be robbed.

'The railway cart is a thing few people remember today – most stations had at least one, because when the parcels arrived by train they had to be delivered round the town and we used a horse and cart.'

Stan's memories of that first job remind us just how little country stations had changed since Stan's great-great-grandfather started work in 1840. Burgess Hill in 1938, and from then until well into the 1950s, still had a full complement of staff because it was felt that the passengers and their needs must come first. Apart from the stationmaster, there were two clerks, two porter-signalmen and the carter: a minimum of six at the kind of station that is now often unmanned. Small stations were also like post offices, selling stamps and collecting parcels, which is why Stan's grandfather managed to combine the roles of stationmaster and postmaster.

'You needed the manpower because you were always busy,' recalls Stan. 'Every train arrived with passengers and parcels in those days, and then there was the van train which came once a day entirely loaded with parcels. Despite there being six staff there was no time for sitting around – the signal boxes were only open in the rush hour or when the goods yard was open, but the signalmen worked as porters carrying parcels, helping passengers and so on.'

Stan just missed being one of the last of the top-hatted stationmasters, but he still wore a smart cap or, on special occasions, a bowler hat. The top hat had been a symbol of the stationmaster's importance and standing in the local community.

'Oh, they were like gods,' says Stan. 'If the stationmaster found me having a quiet fag when I was a junior clerk he'd just take it off me and put it out. Discipline was very strict.'

In August 1939 Stan, a TA soldier, received his call-up papers. At eighteen he was still too young to be sent on active service, so while his battalion, the Royal Sussex, fought in France he was sent off to South Wales to learn to be a radar mechanic.

'I also got married during this period and was posted all over Britain at various times. I was relieved that radar work meant I escaped the infantry, but I was also pleased to get back to civvy street six years later. And the railway, of course, kept my job open.'

After a refresher course Stan went back to work as a booking clerk, but he'd always had a hankering for a stationmaster's job and with his background it must have seemed only a matter of time.

'My first move was to become a relief clerk. This gave you a lot more experience of different stations because you were sent all over the place – wherever they needed you when the regular station clerk was sick or on leave. As a relief clerk you got paid more too because there was a ten per cent allowance for travel. Eventually I put in for a stationmaster's job. You had to go on what was called the stationmaster's panel, which was basically a list of men who were saying they wanted to be a stationmaster. Then when a job came up, the top brass had plenty to choose from. I went through a three-hour test to see if I knew the rules and regulations. I passed and got my first stationmaster's job at Milbourne Port, near Sherbourne, in the West Country.'

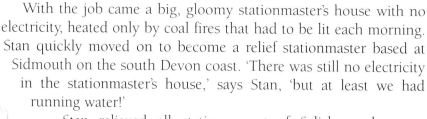

With the job came a big, gloomy stationmaster's house with no electricity, heated only by coal fires that had to be lit each morning. Stan quickly moved on to become a relief stationmaster based at Sidmouth on the south Devon coast. 'There was still no electricity in the stationmaster's house,' says Stan, 'but at least we had running water!'

Stan relieved all stations west of Salisbury down to Axminster in Devon, including Exeter and Barnstaple, and Bude and Padstow in Cornwall. When he had to take over at Padstow it took four hours to get there and four back.

'In those distant West Country towns agriculture was still the big thing. Much of the work of the stationmaster was making sure the cattle trains were loaded, but there was also a lot of horse traffic, and we had the milk trains and sugar beet, and gloves and shirts from Crewkerne and Yeovil because there were big manufacturers in those areas – all now gone, of course.

'The West Country people were very nice to us incomers, but they teased us a bit and I quickly realized that the one thing you couldn't do was hurry them.'

Stan believes that the beginning of the end for the railways as the major freight and parcel carrier came with the ASLEF strike of 1954. Many of the businesses that were forced to use road transport during the strike never returned to the railways.

Transferred back to Brighton in the mid-1950s, Stan worked as relief stationmaster on the London Victoria to Eastbourne line. His strongest memory of this period is the number of derailments and the perils of single-line working.

'Derailments – minor ones – were quite common. There might be an earth slip, or a bit of defective track, or a train would just break down. The stationmaster then had to appoint a pilot man who worked under the signalman at either end of the section and he would get on the footplate of any train that had to come through. In those days we'd probably only take two or three hours to clear an obstruction or sort out a derailment. You had the manpower to see that it was done, and done quickly.'

In 1962 Stan was appointed assistant stationmaster at London Bridge, an extremely busy station even judging by the hectic standards of the day. There were some 1,900 daily train movements through the station, and it was business as usual twenty-four hours a day, seven days a week.

'We had fish trains to the south coast, newspapers, the mail – everything you could think of – and a huge staff. On the portering side alone there were several dozen men.'

Restless as ever, and eager to get on, Stan took a job two years later as relief stationmaster, but he was now on the top grade. He relieved down as far as Eastbourne from his home station at Norwood Junction in South London. Then in 1965 he took over the full stationmaster's job at Redhill in Surrey.

'Most of the work here was routine,' he explains, 'but it had its more gruesome aspect. We often found suicides on the track because we were quite close to two large mental hospitals. In fact in my day Redhill was notorious for suicides.'

Stan is keen to emphasize that the stationmaster's role was at least partly to do with inspiring confidence in the passengers. He had to visit the signal boxes at least once each day and make sure he was out on the platforms every morning during rush hour in case there were complaints or queries.

'I got to know the passengers well because they knew who I was and were happy to talk to me. If they felt you knew what you were talking about – and stationmasters always commanded a degree of respect – they would accept your explanation for any problems. These days I think passengers often get rather hot under the collar because when they ask a member of staff about something they're never quite sure that they're getting a straight answer from someone who really knows what he's talking about.'

Redhill was a busy station and the main postal sorting office for Kent and Sussex. 'Some mornings you couldn't get on the platform for parcels,' says Stan. 'But Redhill was also known as Stopham Junction because it still had old semaphore signalling and it was always going wrong!'

When the signalling or anything else failed there was a good chance that the stationmaster would be called out, whatever the time.

'Well, we had no set hours really – we were supposed to adjust our hours, to use the official phrase, "according to the exigencies of service". So we made our own hours. It could be arduous. On average I was called out once a month in the middle of the night – you were on call twenty-four hours a day on alternate days, which is why you were expected to live on or near the job. Mind you, I shouldn't complain too much because stationmasters did have a few perks – for example, the porters who lit the coal fires in the platform waiting rooms always lit the stationmaster's fire first, and it was still known as a "top-hat job" even if the top hats themselves had gone!'

After five years at Redhill, Stan put in for the job of deputy stationmaster at King's Cross and, sadly, that coincided with the beginning of the end for the traditional position of stationmaster.

'They were starting to introduce the idea of area managers instead of stationmasters, and to be frank I just didn't like the new system. At King's

Stan on the day of his retirement

Cross at first my job was pretty much as it had always been, with masses of local suburban trains to deal with as well as long-distance trains, sleepers and the usual freight. The thing about being a stationmaster is that you had to be aware of everything that was going on at the same time. But once I became an operations manager I became remote from the station staff because I no longer looked after the station – I was responsible for a much bigger area, from King's Cross up to Wood Green some miles away. But I did twelve years and then took early retirement. What strikes me most about my years on the railway is how much change took place – I reckon far more changed over my forty years than over the previous century. I saw the freight disappear, I saw all the signal boxes go and, of course, I saw the end of the job that five generations of my family had been proud to carry out.'

A late nineteenth-century steam locomotive

Pages 106–7 Courtesy of Milepost 92½ Picture Library

Head banger

'Put your head inside, sir,' shouted the guard to a passenger who was leaning far out of the window as a train steamed out of the station. 'I shall do as I like,' retorted the passenger. 'All right,' was the reply. 'Do as you please, but you must understand that you'll be held liable for all damage done to the stonework of the company's bridges.'
Our Best Railway Stories, 1900

Coaches from London

Only eleven mail coaches now leave London daily for the country. A few years since, before the railways were formed there were nearly eighty that used to leave the general post office.
The Times, 1843

Rail making

Unfortunately, as the metal is improved, the increase of weight on the wheels seems to counterbalance the improvement. These considerations naturally lead to the comparison of iron and steel as the material for rails; and in considering the distinctive characteristics of the two materials, the mode of manufacture of each must be borne in mind.

An iron rail is made by rolling together a number of separate pieces of iron, which, when placed ready for rolling, are called the rail pile. It is of much consequence in designing rails, or indeed any other form of rolled iron, that all parts of the section should be such as to be suitable to being rolled at one or nearly one intensity of heat. Area differences of thickness in the section are to be avoided as much as possible, for the heat which is suitable for the thick portions may be so high as to cause the thin portions to be unduly yielding.

A rail pile is composed in different ways according to the specifications of engineers and the price of the rails. Speaking generally the pile is made about 8½in wide and 9in high, and if the rail to be rolled is a double-headed rail, it is built up as follows.

The part of the pile which will hereafter form the two heads of the rail consists of slabs of hard hammered iron 8½in wide, and 2¼in thick, and the space between the slabs is filled

Second class on the railway, Epsom Races, 1847

up with puddle bars ¾in thick, which may either be as wide as the pile, or may be put together so as to break joint. The pile is heated in a furnace to a welding heat, and hammered or rolled into a solid lump or bloom, about 5in wide, and 6in deep which is again heated to a welding heat and rolled into the finished rail.

Railway Appliances, J. W. Barry, 1884

Signals communication

There are two needles for each line in each signal box, which are painted respectively red and black. The black needle shows the last signal received at any signal box, and the red needle shows the last signal sent from the same signal box. Thus a signalman has before him not only the order sent to him from a distant signal box, but also a record of the order which he himself has last sent to the other signal box. The black needles can only be affected by currents of electricity sent from another signal box, and the signalman in whose box they are placed cannot alter their position.

It will be observed that there is a seeming contradiction in this system of signalling, in the signalman at B replying to the request of the signalman at A for permission to send a train, by saying on the bell signal, 'Yes, send the train,' but turning the needle at the same time to the prohibitory signal of 'Train on line'.

This contradiction is more apparent than real, and is not found to lead to mistakes in working. The important part of the block system is to promptly block the line behind a train to prevent another following it till the first train gets clear of the next station, and it is better to do this even before the first train passes than to delay the signal for the time necessary to send another signal to say the train has passed.

Railway Appliances, J. W. Barry, 1884

Slow train

TICKET COLLECTOR AT DESTINATION STATION: 'This boy has travelled on a child's ticket – surely, Madam, he is over twelve years of age.'

MADAM (who has arrived by the slow train): 'Maybe he is, but he was only eleven when we started.'

Our Best Railway Stories, 1900

The joys of steam travel

The judges, sent down as a Special Commission to try some rioters at Stafford, went by special train from Euston. It would appear, therefore, says the *Railway Times,* that travelling by railway is not now considered beneath the dignity of the profession.

On the other hand, Lord Abinger, presiding in the Court of Exchequer, said that it would be a great tyranny if the Court were to lay down that a witness should only travel by railway. If he were a witness, he insisted, in the present state of railways, he should refuse to come by such a conveyance.

Perhaps Lord Abinger and Louis Philippe's ministers might be forgiven if they were disinclined to accept the present state of railways as altogether satisfactory. Here is what Mr Bourne, a professed panegyrist of the new system, describes as a typical experience as late as the beginning of 1846:

'It requires perhaps some boldness to claim for a mere piece of machinery, a combination of wheels and pistons, familiar to us by frequent use, any alliance with the sublime. Let the reader, however, place himself in imagination upon the margin of one of those broad dales of England, such for example as that of Barnsley in Yorkshire, of Stafford, or the vale of Berks, in each of which a great passenger railway is carried, and over which the eye commands an extended view.

Credit: National Railway Museum/Science & Society

No 3 SAFE SANDS

EAST COAST JOYS
travel by L·N·E·R
TO THE DRIER SIDE OF BRITAIN

LISHED BY THE LONDON & NORTH EASTERN RAILWAY   HAYCOCK PRESS, LONDON.

'In the extreme distance a white line of cloud appears to rise from the ground, and gradually passes away into the atmosphere. Soon a light murmur falls upon the ear, and the glitter of polished metal appears from time to time among the trees. The murmur soon becomes deeper and more tremulous. The cloud rises of a more fleecy whiteness, and its conversion into the transparent air is more evident. The train rushes on; the bright engine rolls into full view; now crossing the broad river, now threading the various bendings of the railway, followed by its dark serpent-like body.

'The character of the sound is changed. The pleasant murmur becomes a deep intermitting boom, the clank of chains and carriage-fastenings is heard, and the train rolls along the rails with a resonance like thunder.

'Suddenly a wagon stands in the way, or a plank, it may be, has been left across the rails; a shrill, unearthly scream issues from the engine, piercing the ears of the offending workmen, and scarcely less alarming the innocent passengers. Many a foolish head is popped out of the window, guards and brakesmen busily apply their drags, and the driver reverses the machinery of his engine, and exerts its utmost force, though in vain, to stop the motion. The whole mass fairly slides upon the rail with the momentum due to some 60 or 70 tons.

'Then comes the moment of suspense, when nothing remains to be done, and it is uncertain whether the obstacle will be removed in time, It is so; and the huge mass slides by with scarcely an inch to spare. Off go the brakes, round fly the wheels, the steam is again turned on, and the train rolls forward at its wonted speed, until smoothly and silently it glides into the appointed stopping-place. Then come the opening of doors, and the bustle of luggage-porters. Coaches, cabs, omnibuses, vehicles of every description, fill and rapidly drive off, until before ten minutes have elapsed the uncouth engine has slunk back into its house, and some hundred passengers, with their luggage, have disappeared like a dream, and the platform is once more left to silence and solitude.'

The Railways of England, W. M. Acworth, 1889

Making the farmers angry

At last one or two strange faces appeared in the town, and men in leather leggings, dragging a long chain, and attended by one or two country labourers armed with bill-hooks, were remarked as trespassing in the most unwarrantable manner over pasture land, standing crops, copse and cover; actually cutting gaps in the hedges, through which they climbed and dragged the land-chain.

Then would follow another intruder, bearing a telescope set on three legs, which he erected with the most perfect coolness wherever he thought fit, peering through it at a long white staff, marked with unintelligible hieroglyphics, which was borne by another labourer, and moved or held stationary in accordance

with a mysterious code of telegraphic signals made by the hand.

The farmers, naturally indignant, ordered these intruders from their fields. The engineers, for such they were, took but little notice. The farmers proceeded to threats. The ringleader of the invaders produced a red notebook, folded in an oblong form, from the voluminous pocket of his velveteen jacket, and offered it to the irate farmer as a sedative, informing him that it was the Act of Parliament by authority of which he was acting, and further specifying that it was a King's printer's copy of the Act, and therefore was legal evidence. The farmers, at their wits' ends, did all in their power to rout and baffle the intruders, but in vain. One thing alone remained for them to do – and often they positively swore that they would have recourse to that extreme step – they would

shoot the intruders. But the latter calmly replied that that was no business of theirs, and the farmers did not draw the trigger. The blank look of petrified astonishment which crept over the furious face of an irate farmer, when his threat of instant death, enforced by the production of a weapon, was met by the calm rejoinder that the result was his lookout, and not that of his tormentor, would have been a fine study for a great comedian. It was so ridiculous as to be almost sublime.

The next step in the invasion proved a yet further aggravation to the farmers, although it was one which, for the first time in the course of the contest, afforded them the pleasure of retaliation. Loads of oak pegs, accurately squared, painted and pointed, were driven to the fields, and the course of the intended railway was marked out by driving two of these pegs, one left standing about four inches above the surface to indicate position, and a smaller one driven lower to the ground a few inches off on which to take the level, at every interval of twenty-two yards. It is obvious that the operations of farming afforded many an opportunity for an unfriendly blow at these pegs. Ploughs and harrows had a remarkable tendency to be come entangled in them; cart wheels ran foul of them; sometimes they disappeared altogether.

A mute and irregular warfare on the subject of the pegs was generally protracted until the last outrage was perpetrated by the agents of the company; the land was purchased for the railway.

Personal Recollections of English Engineers, F. R. Conder, 1868

Winding engine at Euston

In the two miles of extension from Camden Town to Euston Square, the engineers had to solve nearly every problem which has subsequently to that time been encountered by the projectors of metropolitan railways. The canal had to be crossed under heavy penalties for interfering with its traffic. The alteration of an inch or two of level in the great highways was a matter of keen debate in committee, and the executive of the parliamentary conditions was closely watched by the courteous vigilance of Sir James MacAdam. The sewers had to be avoided or provided for. Nearly half the bridges that were constructed were insisted on in order to provide for future roads, and intended streets and crescents. The gradients were of what was at that time considered unparalleled severity, so much so that the idea of running trains propelled by locomotives from the terminus was laid aside; a powerful winding engine was erected at Camden Town and a cumbrous but well-considered apparatus of ropes and pullies [sic] was laid down in order to draw the trains up the inclines of 1 in 75 and 1 in 76. The main difficulty which, at this stage of our scientific knowledge, was found to press on the engineers of the line, was the design and construction of a telegraph, which, in all states of the weather, and by night as well as by day, should instantly communicate the orders of the stationmaster at Euston, to the enginemen at Camden Town. Mr Wheatstone was then but commencing the experiments which have led to the perfect solution of a problem, impracticable to science without the aid of electricity.

The first efforts made in the study which has led to our present Atlantic cables, were directed to the transmission of musical tones through wires.
Personal Recollections of English Engineers, F. R. Conder, 1868

A very late train indeed

The train was very late. There was no disputing that fact. The stationmaster was endeavouring to pacify the aggrieved passenger and explained how circumstances beyond the control of the railway company were responsible for the delay, and that a little time lost here and there on the journey had aggregated in the train's late arrival at its destination. He then proceeded to demonstrate by his watch, which recorded Greenwich Mean Time, that the train was not so late after all as the complainant made out.

But the man who missed his appointment was not to be appeased, for his final retort was: 'You can't explain it that way, my man. What you want is a calendar, not a watch, for a case of this kind.'
Our Best Railway Stories, 1900

Six of one

The stationmaster was of the pompous old school who would tolerate no other opinion than his own and was always right. A dispute had arisen as to the damage of some goods conveyed by train. The sender declared the breakages were due to the carelessness of the porter handling them, whilst the porter was highly indignant at the suggestion and called attention to the fact that the box was badly packed. 'I expect, if the truth's known,' said the booking clerk, putting in his oar, 'it was six of one and half-a-dozen of the other.'

'You weren't asked for your opinion, Mr Jenkins,' snapped the stationmaster, irascibly. 'And as it happens, you're quite wrong – it was just the opposite.'
Our Best Railway Stories, 1900

Rail surveyors in the schoolyard

It may readily be supposed that the indignant astonishment with which county owners and occupiers regarded the authorized trespass of the railway pioneers, was not greater than that evinced by metropolitan and suburban residents. Not rarely has it occurred for a respectable inhabitant of Mornington Crescent to find the peace of his family disturbed by the announcement, that strange men were clambering over his garden wall; and on sallying forth, indignant, to demand the reason of the intrusion, to find them coolly engaged, with hammers and cold chisels, in boring a hole through the wall of his toolhouse or summer-house.

One sufferer in particular discharged many torrents of fiery indignation on the devoted heads of Mr Stephenson's staff.

Public sympathy, it is to be feared, would even now rather be on the side of the residents than on that of the intruders. The gentleman in question was a schoolmaster, and eminent for that high respect for his own personal dignity which, from the days of Dionysius to those of Dr Parr, all independent educators and chastisers of youth have been known to cherish. His school was not large, but it appeared to be respectable, and his house was rendered more attractive by the presence of a sprightly black-eyed daughter. It so chanced that this house occupied a corner of one of the great roads crossed by the railway; and that an annex of one storey, a hall or a breakfast room, with a flat leaded roof, lay in the very centre line. To complete the survey on the large scale of 80 inches to the mile, which was the first duty of the staff when the Act for the Euston Extension had received the Royal Assent, it was necessary repeatedly to invade this gentleman's premises, to cut holes in his garden-wall, and to make use of his very convenient 'leads' as a station for the theodolite.

For the sake of convenience and despatch, the surveying party always carried a short and handy ladder; and as the Act of Parliament authorized entrance on all the scheduled property for the purpose of surveying, the orders were to take what is called French leave, to proceed in the most straightforward and rapid manner and to take no notice of occupiers unless they interfered with the survey. Whether this was the most courteous mode of procedure is not the question. It was legal, and it was a great saving of time.

On a calm retrospect of the pros and cons of the question, it seems that courtesy for the most part would have been wasted, and time with it. However that may be, it could hardly have been very agreeable for the worthy tutor to find the window of his schoolroom suddenly darkened, and, on looking up to ascertain the cause, to behold on the leaden flat, immediately outside the room and level

Credit: National Railway Museum/Science & Society

with the floor on which stood, his wondering scholars, a pair of very long legs descending from beneath a blue mackintosh cape. The back of this figure was respectfully presented to the inmates of the house as a sign that no intrusion was intended on their privacy, while the owner of the legs and one or two assistants were carefully fixing a theodolite on the flat, and marking with penknives the exact spot occupied by each of the three legs of the instrument, for the sake of exactitude of dispatch on future occasions.

The window is thrown open; the master, in flowing dressing gown, advances majestically towards the intruders; the amazed schoolboys delighted with the lark crowd in a semi-circle behind him; the half-scared, half-indignant mistress appears at an adjoining window; the pretty daughter makes good use of her fine eyes on the floor above (as is noted by the engineer's pupils); the giggling servants crowd on tiptoe in the yard below.

'Who are you, sir, and how dare you come on my leads?'

'Sir, I am an assistant of Mr Robert Stephenson and I am engaged on a survey for the Euston Grove extension of the London and Birmingham Railway.'

'And what business have you on my premises?'

'The centre line of the railway passes exactly beneath the plumb-bob of my instrument.'

'Don't talk to me of plumb-bobs sir; how dare you climb up there and to have the impertinence to stare in at my windows?'

'If you will have the kindness to look at this book...'

'Don't talk to me of books! I say how dare you come here.'

'That is just what I produced the book to explain sir...'

'What on earth do you mean sir?'

'I mean sir this is the Act of Parliament in virtue of which the officers of the company are authorized to enter on the properties scheduled in the book of reference for the purposes of survey.'

'Hang the officers of the company! And the purposes of survey! And you too sir! Once for all, will you leave my premises directly?'

'I regret that my duty forbids me to do so sir, but we will be as rapid in our work and give you as little annoyance as possible.'

'Then sir I shall instantly send for a policeman.'

'Perhaps that will be the most satisfactory course sir. The policeman will no doubt convince you we are only doing our duty.'

Grand tableau! Young people seem most highly to appreciate the fun. Doctor retreats to send for the police.

Personal Recollections of English Engineers, F. R. Conder, 1868

First class on the railway, Epsom Races, 1847

THE MAN WITH THE EMPIRE MEDAL

RON WEEKS,
FIREMAN AND DRIVER

Ron Weeks' first job in the late 1930s was driving a massive World War I lorry for the Royal Arsenal Co-op. The job sticks in his mind because when he was reversing or manoeuvring the lorry slowly round a corner he had to stand up to turn the wheel, but it was all part of a tough apprenticeship that gave him a head start when he joined the railways a few years later.

Ron now lives with his son in Gillingham on the north Kent coast. A Londoner born and bred, he moved out of 'the Smoke' in 1968, some twenty years before he retired.

'I was born in 1923 and grew up in Highbury. Then we went south of the river to Brixton. For a couple of years after I left school I worked delivering firewood, and then in 1941 I got that job driving the old lorries after failing my call-up medical on account of lung trouble. They were murder. Apart from the incredibly heavy steering, we had to double de-clutch the damn things – hardly anyone remembers that now. You had to use the clutch to put the thing in neutral each time you changed gear. Having put it in neutral you let out the clutch, then pushed it back in before selecting your new gear.'

The completely unsealed lorry cabs meant drivers were continually exposed to exhaust and diesel fumes and, rather than become ill, Ron decided to pack it in.

'I drove round London delivering all sorts of things until 1946 – right through the war years in fact, but it was affecting my health, so I looked around and thought – I know, I'll join the railways. I applied to Stewart's Lane, went to London Bridge for a medical and to my surprise passed. So I got a job on the Great Southern Railway but based at Stewart's Lane, Battersea.'

Stewart's Lane, one of the biggest locomotive sheds in the area, was incredibly busy when Ron started work.

'When you think how big it was it seems strange to think that it's all gone now – not a trace of it left. But when I joined there were twelve gangs of twelve men each, plus the shedmaster who was in charge of the whole thing. His boss – the supervisor – only turned up every now and then. Stewart's Lane covered steam work right round the south and south-east – Folkestone, Dover, and then across to Portsmouth.'

Like all footplate men Ron started as a cleaner and worked his way up. As he points out, there was nothing romantic about engine cleaning because cleaners were effectively the lowest of the low, but they were at least on the bottom rung of the promotion ladder.

'It was the only way to get in,' he recalls. 'And it wasn't just that you cleaned the engines because you were useless for anything else. Cleaning an engine is the best

way to get a basic understanding of how it works. We didn't just hose the things down, either, which is probably what they'd do now – we had to climb in and around every bit of the motion work, the boiler, the firebox. And those old steam locos were cleaned by us boys every time they came into the shed. There would be a cleaner foreman and three or four cleaners, and you had to do the equivalent of a year's cleaning before you could even start as a fireman. We just had old overalls which we had to wash ourselves at home, but they got so dirty I suppose they were hardly ever

LNER Class B1 4-6-0, circa 1945. Credit: National Railway Museum/Science & Society

completely clean. The most junior cleaner did the very dirtiest bits right underneath the engine, but when he'd gained a bit of seniority he might get to do the boiler which was a lot cleaner.

'I would have been about twenty-three at this time, and like all railway workers we had to do shifts – early, middle and late – and the foreman was very particular about how we cleaned. He'd send you back to do it again if it wasn't right, so you'd all try to brush up every bit of it.

'When we were cleaning one of the Royal Trains – there were four of them in those days, I think – the shedmaster would check absolutely everything, right down to the rivets. We also did the Derby Day trains and they were very particular about those, too! For the Royal trains they always used an engine that had just been serviced – couldn't take any risks. Imagine the embarrassment if that broke down!'

As a passed cleaner Ron got his hat, badge and lightweight coat – the symbols of success and his gaining the next rung of the ladder.

'I was so proud when I got my hat and badge. I loved wearing my uniform every day. It was a dark-blue serge – quite rough material and probably pretty much what railwaymen had worn since the nineteenth century. Officially it should have been renewed yearly – but I hardly ever remember that happening.

'After that first year you carried on cleaning, but you were always hoping that somewhere in the shed someone would be short of a fireman and grab you. But there's a bit of a myth about the old boys who drove the engines at that time. People talk about them as if they were all masters of the art of steam-train driving, but it's not true at all. Some of them were right old rogues – some could hardly drive at all. They'd just open the regulator and thrash the life out of the engine. I think it was us youngsters who wanted to make driving more of an art, something we took pride in.'

Most of the drivers Ron worked with in the early days would have been 1918 men who would have learned their driving from the Victorians. But the basic skills remained the same, even if not everyone bothered to stick to them. Ron was a stickler for carrying out even basic tasks properly, as he explains.

'When you started your shift you collected your tools from the store room – your oil can, shovel, bucket and spanners. I then always used to check the smokebox because all the vibration from previous journeys meant that it regularly came loose. If it was I'd make sure it was nicely tightened before we set off, otherwise I knew we'd lose heat and power.'

Like most footplate men who developed a real love for their craft, Ron recalls his first day's firing as if it were yesterday.

'Oh, I'll never forget it. I was pretty nervous, but really excited as well. I went up to the driver and told him I was his fireman. He said, "How long have you been firing?" When I told him it was my first time he said, "I'm not having you. I'm going

to get someone else" – and he did. So after all that excitement it was a bit of a let-down, but the older men could be like that. They weren't all helpful or even friendly.'

But after that false start Ron began to get plenty of firing turns. He reckons it was because drivers could tell that he was hungry for work, but also keen to do the job well.

'I took an interest, and I began to notice that the good drivers didn't just thrash the engine by opening the regulator. They'd be checking the boiler pressure, and using the injectors and the regulator together. And those good drivers took an interest in me because they knew I wanted to get on.

'We had some very good engines, but like most people I remember the Southern Pacifics that hauled the *Golden Arrow* as particularly good locomotives. We also had some pretty lousy ones – like most sheds we had the greatest number of problems with the old goods engines because they were badly maintained.'

Ron was 'on the shovel', as he puts it, from 1947 until 1954, and all that time he was learning the roads, learning the rules and regulations and, most important, learning how to drive. Occasionally a driver would let him take over and have a go at driving.

'That's the big difference between then and now. In the old days you learned thoroughly because you had the time to do it. Drivers can't do that now because they're rushed through the system. That's why they go through red lights and cause these terrible accidents.

'Firing was important because you were helping make the engine run well, and all the time you knew you were getting closer to being a driver. And there were always a few men who were really good at helping each other, or who wanted to get together with their mates to learn more about the job.'

In 1949 Ron helped set up a club for firemen waiting to become drivers. The plan was to teach them about how the various locomotives worked, how to steam, the names of all the parts of the engine and the details of the rule book.

'We weren't expected to know the rule book off by heart, but we did need to know it well because we were tested on it. Through the classes I set up we helped train more than fifty men, and they all went on to be good drivers. All that self-help work outside work hours was voluntary – none of the men got paid for it. Can you imagine saying to railwaymen today that you'd like them to go for training every week, but that they won't get paid for it? There'd be a riot!'

By this time Ron was also beginning to get interested in the social side of railway work, a move that was to lead to decades of voluntary work with the railwaymen's union, ASLEF. But it all started with the realization that little was done for railwaymen and their families outside working hours.

'Well, till we started to do something about it, almost nothing ever happened in the way of social get-togethers. Then my wife and I started to help with the social section, organizing retirement functions, and parties for children at Christmas, and we realized that the younger men had almost nothing to do with the older men so we arranged outings where they could get together. And they were very popular.'

The very nature of railway work made socializing difficult. There was a drivers'

lobby where the men would sit by a big fire in their time between jobs, but they might stop at odd times which meant bumping into men from other links only occasionally.

'Footplate men didn't all stop together for lunch at 1pm like office workers,' explains Ron. 'You just stopped whenever you had a break. It could be any time. We all had old lockers in the lobby and tins to keep our stuff in – lots of the men had old gas-mask cases. They preferred them to the tins we were issued with. But other men had their own cases – all sorts. I carried my gear in an old leather doctor's bag. A Dr Johnson case I used to call it.'

Ron's interest in the social side of railway life didn't detract from his determination to get on. He learned the fireman's job inside out, and even today his memory of a typical morning in the shed is meticulous.

'When you were a fireman you didn't usually have to start the engine from cold. The fire raisers would do that before you arrived. They knew when each engine had to be ready and they went round lighting them up as and when – terrible job, really, very dirty, but at least it meant that men who'd failed to pass for driving, maybe because they'd lost an eye or for whatever reason, had work. Anyway, we booked on and were then told what we were going to do. All you knew was the time to be there. Of course the shifts changed every day, but we tried to keep on one shift if we could.

'The fireman's first job was to go to the oil store for what we called the blackpot – that was the heavy oil for the motion work. It was so heavy we had to warm it first in front of the firebox door! Oiling was the responsibility of the driver, but the fireman would help. Once the oiling had been done you'd rake over the fire to make sure there wasn't too much smoke. Then you'd get the pressure up and report to the yard foreman. He had to be told that you wanted to leave the shed so he could set the signals.

'Then it was time to go. Too much smoke from your fire would mean trouble – the smoke jacks would come round and tell you off because the smoke in the shed was terrible even at the best of times because there were so many engines and fires. One or two engines producing a lot of smoke because the fire wasn't being attended to properly could make it almost unbearable. We used to put the blower on to reduce the amount of smoke.

'Different engines went out under different pressures, but one thing is certain – you wouldn't move an inch without plenty of steam, and you wouldn't be able to stop either because the brakes were steam-operated.'

Ron's dominant memory of his firing days is of how much he enjoyed them; not just because he felt he was progressing in his career, but also because he had become immersed in the friendships and friendly rivalries between the men. Work and work-related free time took over more and more of his life, but in 1955 came the great day he'd been waiting for: he was passed for driving.

'I felt I'd really arrived when I was no longer just a fireman, but a fireman available for driving duties. Mind you, I wasn't what they called an "appointed driver". That took a lot longer and you had to put in for it. You passed for driving as a fireman when you'd done your turns – in other words when, as a fireman, you'd managed to do a year's worth of turns.

'The day after I passed for driving I was due to come in and work on the Sunday morning. I arrived, booked on and went to see the foreman. I told him I was the 10am spare. I waited in the lobby while he went off about his business. Then he came back whistling "The Blue Bells of Scotland". Can't imagine why I remember that, but I do. I suppose it was because I was nervous as this was my first time as a driver with full responsibility. Anyway, the foreman said that a driver was needed on the 10am to Dover. And that was it. I was away. The whole thing was quite scary, but we'd been trained for ten or twelve years for this and I knew every inch of the road to Dover. I can remember thinking, "I know this road, I know where the restrictions and speed limits are" – and there were lots of them. Also there was a fair bit of hill climbing so I knew I had to make sure the fireman kept up a good head of steam. You'd pick up steam on the way downhill so you'd have the momentum to get over the top of the next hill. Drivers did get that sort of thing wrong now and then and would just grind to a halt and lose time.'

A permanent way gang photographed during track maintenance, 1912. Credit: National Railway Museum/Science & Society

'Driving was great. In the autumn you could enjoy all the colours of the trees and the countryside along the track side; in summer it was usually comfortable on the footplate because you were open to the air; in winter the fire would mean you kept reasonably warm. Of course on a very hot day in summer you might sweat a bit, and in winter if you were going tender-first it was always bloody freezing because all the weather just came right in on top of you.

'On that first day when I drove to Dover one of the men I'd trained in the volunteer classes fired for me, and in fact we became great friends and kept in touch for years. But that was and is a key thing about the railways – the friends you made then were friends for life as often as not. I've been retired for more than ten years, but I still see all my old mates – those that haven't passed away – regularly. We really were and are like a big family and, OK, you might not get on with one or two, but generally you were all in the same boat so you supported each other.

'I loved it when people said, "You're a bit young to be an train driver". I remember going to Victoria station in London to hook on a train, and as we set off I felt ten feet tall being in charge of the whole thing. It did make you a bit big-headed, I suppose! And people often came along the platform to talk to the driver, or they'd ask if they could come up on the footplate. Children loved it, but I don't remember it ever happening once we went over to diesel.'

But as Ron's driving career progressed he found he was working even harder – but as a volunteer – on the social side.

'Oh, my house down in Brixton was like a railway open house – every Thursday all the drivers came round, maybe as many of eighteen, plus all their future wives. We ran those Thursdays for years, my wife and me, till the end of steam. Nothing like that had been done before. It was a great achievement and widely recognized.'

Ron moved out of the rat race and London life in 1968 to a long, sunny street in Gillingham, overlooking the wide expanse of the Thames estuary. Meanwhile, on the Southern Region, steam had all but vanished by the mid-1960s. Ron continued to drive as a passed fireman until he was appointed to the dual link at Stewart's Lane, Battersea, working on steam and electric.

'I used to escort drivers who were much older than me across the difficult sections of road. One elderly chap I conducted through Crystal Palace (a very different route) got fed up with the whole thing and started thrashing the engine, so I tried diplomatically to tell him how to do it. I got so fed up with the way he was driving I even fired for him.'

One of the biggest problems for railwaymen was how little provision there was for their retirement. So men like Ron, helped by others, set up railwaymen's pension and welfare funds. 'I became chairman of the Railwayman's Local Pension Fund, which we set up for ourselves, and I ran it until it shut down when bigger companies got involved.'

Some of the old benefit organizations had wonderful names. Ron was chairman of both the Railway Companies' Servants' Sick and Benefit Society and the Death Injury and Provision Society.

'It was a very interesting time. Every week I used to go through Stewart's Lane for union funds and sick calls,' he recalls. 'If any man became sick he'd get help, but the men also rallied round in an informal way to offer help. None of us had a lot of money, but we did what we could.'

Ron continued to travel up to Victoria from Gillingham every day until he retired in 1988. His memories of his working days centre mostly around the men he worked with, but he has fond memories too of the actual locomotives.

'At the Festival of Britain Exhibition in 1952, on London's South Bank, the Standard engine 70014 was shown off as the latest in steam technology. It was a marvellous engine, but with the advent of electricity and diesel it was scrapped, along with other fine designs, before it ever really had a chance to show what it could do. A lot of individual engines were scrapped without being used even once!'

Ron still enjoys seeing the preserved Southern Pacifics that come through Gillingham on special steam train days. 'They couldn't quite kill them off completely,' he says with a grin. 'People like them too much.'

Like most railwaymen Ron remembers odd accidents and mistakes. 'I was firing

on what turned into a runaway coal train. The engine couldn't control the weight, but it wasn't the driver's fault. We should have had two locos on that train – in other words, it should have been a double-header – but we only had one and we stopped about 2 miles further on than we should have done. I knew we should have gone out with two locos because when we started off we could hardly get the thing moving. We could see the guard on the train that ran into us after we'd gone past the signal. He was desperately trying to screw down the brake, but his train was very heavy as it had wagons filled with rails, which weighed an incredible amount. There was no way he was going to stop. Anyway, there was a terrific bang and we got covered with coal – it came pouring over us from the tender.

'On another occasion I had a near miss. We were just coming into Balham station in South London and I said to the fireman, "Can you pray?" "Why?" he said. "Because we've had it," I replied. I hadn't had the steam to stop my train and we'd passed a red light. There was a train coming towards us and if it had hit us we'd have had a hell of a smash. Luckily it came on and passed us by on the other track – that was a lucky escape.'

Ron had started as assistant secretary of the Battersea branch of the drivers' union, ASLEF, a few years after starting work and just after the previous incumbent had left the railway service. By 1948 he was ASLEF secretary at Battersea, and he was to remain in that post almost for the rest of his career.

'We were never paid but I didn't mind about that. I wanted to help and I was well organized. I liked doing it. If a chap died we'd offer to sort out his estate and help his wife. I can remember my first job for ASLEF – a young fireman called John Perry, a really nice bloke, had been killed in a motorcycle accident at Beckenham. John had money in various clubs, but his mum and dad were so upset they didn't want it. I went to see them and we put the money in a fund for John's sister. The parents were happy with that. John's dad was so pleased he sent me a gold pen with my name on it. I've never forgotten that and I still have the pen.'

Ron was ASLEF branch secretary for thirty-seven years. Industrial relations were generally pretty good – despite press coverage that suggested otherwise – but Ron does recall the nationwide strike of 1955.

'It was a strike over pay, but no one really won. I had to go round in the middle of the night with Reg Coote and make sure the pickets were OK. At that time the police were helpful and supportive of what we were trying to do. When it was over and we went back to work firemen got another 1/- [5p] a week. Drivers got a bit more.

'One of the funniest things I remember is how often right through my time men would come in to sign on for work on days when they were on holiday! I never quite knew whether it was just forgetfulness and force of habit, or whether they just didn't want to stay at home with nothing to do.'

Ron finally left Battersea in 1968 and started working at Victoria station. He was still driving, but by now it was almost all electric and diesel.

Lines of communication: King's Cross station, 1938. Credit: National Railway Museum/Science & Society

'There was a bit of steam left, but not much. I didn't realize how much I missed it until it was completely gone. By the late 1960s we had diesels on the Uckfield line and electrics to Portsmouth, Brighton and Deal. I missed steam because you always had something to do or something to check or adjust. It was an art, and that certainly wasn't true of diesels and electrics. On steam the fireman might really have to fight to get enough steam.'

After nearly forty years' service, Ron's name was put forward for the British Empire Medal for Services to British Railways in 1979. He went with his wife and family to Hever Castle in Kent where the Lord Lieutenant of the County presented him with the rare honour.

'I was quite pleased when he said he wondered – with all the work I did in ASLEF – how I was ever at home at all!

'My only regret today is that the railways have got into such a mess – all they're interested in now is trying to make money.'

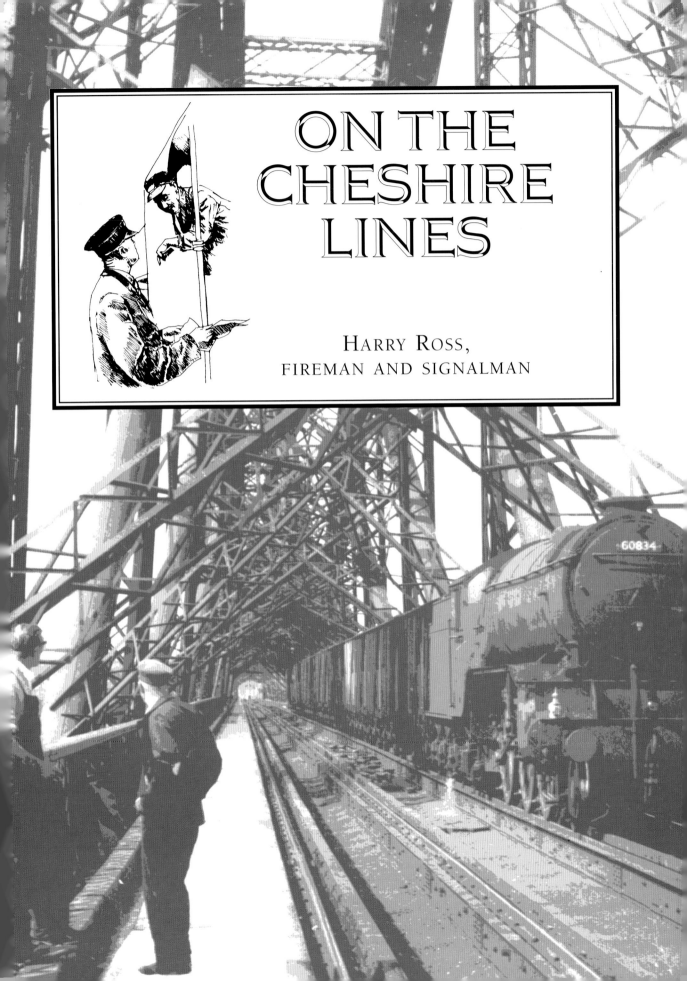

ON THE CHESHIRE LINES

HARRY ROSS,
FIREMAN AND SIGNALMAN

Harry Ross has an almost encyclopaedic knowledge of railways in general, and his own career – which lasted almost fifty years – in particular. Having grown up in a house where railway work was a central part of everyday life, it was no surprise when Harry started work at Chester in 1935 as a junior porter. Harry's father was a driver on the Great Western, and his grandfather had been a station inspector at Chester General station.

'That was a really important station in those days,' says Harry with a smile. 'And we're probably talking about the 1900s or earlier. The stationmaster wore a top hat and walked around the station as if he really meant business.'

Harry was born in 1920, but age hasn't diminished his memories or his sense of humour. Wonderful anecdotes and detailed information about the days of steam working spill out of him as he talks in the sitting room of his immaculately tidy semi in Salford, Greater Manchester. As he explains, it was just the same when he was a schoolboy: born as he was into a railway family, all the talk was of railways.

'The fact that I had relatives in the business made a difference when it came to trying to get in,' he says. 'My grandfather had probably started work in the 1860s or 70s, and my father was certainly on the footplate before the Great War. Railway work, you could say, was in my blood.'

Harry's father volunteered for service in World War I and fought in Egypt, and then returned to his old job as a driver. By the early 1930s Harry was keen to join him, but no sooner had he started that junior porter's job at Chester than he was made redundant. 'I'd only been there six months – it was a hell of a shock!'

However, he was told that if a vacancy occurred he'd be contacted. And that's what happened. When news of the second job reached him Harry discovered he was to work on the weighbridge at Chester.

'Weighbridge says it all – sounds mad today, but we were actually weighing coal lorries. We weighed them before they were loaded with coal, and then again afterwards, and the difference gave us the amount of coal they were carrying. The coalmen who'd bought the coal and were to sell it on to houses and shops and pubs in Chester were allowed so many days to empty the wagon – rail wagon, that is. But if they hadn't emptied it by the end of the allotted time they were charged what was called "demurrage" – a sort of surcharge.'

A few months after this second start, Harry's father managed to get him the opportunity of going to one of the best-known centres of the railway industry: Swindon, the headquarters of the Great Western Railway.

'I was all ready packed and waiting for the off. At Swindon I had a medical – which I thought would be routine – and couldn't believe it when I failed. I was heart-broken and they didn't even make it clear *why* I'd failed. Anyway, a mate of mine said I wasn't to worry as I could join him as a cleaner on the London & North Eastern Railway at Chester, so that's what I did. It was known then as Cheshire Lines Railways, but it was really an arm of the Great Central Section of the LNER. I passed my medical at Gorton in 1937, and took my first step on the road to becoming a driver.'

Like all cleaners in those now distant days, Harry was given a set of overalls, a bundle of rags – known as 'waste' – and a pot of paraffin.

'I remember we used the paraffin to clean the wheels and motion work, and a special creamy sort of oil to do the paintwork sections. We worked in a gang of four, and we'd always toss a coin to see who was going to do the dirtiest job. Cleaning the boiler and tender was probably the plum job, at least in the sense that it was cleanest. For the motion work you'd have to get right under the engine where it was absolutely filthy – right in between the frame and the connecting rods. You can't imagine how black it got in there. Whenever you were cleaning you had to display a "Not to be Moved" board just in case some lunatic tried to move the engine while you were crawling around underneath.

'But all the time we were cleaning what we really wanted was to be on the footplate, and we were always hoping the drivers would let us up there with them. Sometimes, of course, they did get us up there and that's how we began to learn about how the engine worked. But cleaning was definitely an excellent way to get a good understanding of the moving parts and how the whole thing fitted together.'

Cleaning, however, was a slow business – as Harry explains, a gang of four could do just two tank engines in eight hours, and a tender would take longer. At Chester most of the engines were small: 'We had C13 tanks, 4-4-2s, N5s (but not the superheated ones), J10s and the Sentinel Railcar, a passenger car with the engine at one end. It did local trips from Chester Northgate to Shotton.

'As cleaners you had to show you were keen, so we'd help if anyone had to move an engine, and they'd let us help if they needed someone to rake out the ashpan in a locomotive – in other words, clean out the remains of the fire, a very dirty job. We were doing some bits of the work that driver and fireman would normally do, so we never missed a chance. It was all experience. The older lads would also help us and there were what we called Mutual Improvement Classes; they were voluntary, but almost all of us went to them. We'd discuss the rules and regulations, how the engine worked and the brakes, and the details of the various roads we knew we'd eventually have to learn.'

In 1938, Harry passed out as a cleaner. That meant he could officially work firing turns or shifts, though of course, as he's the first to admit, he'd done lots of 'unofficial' firing already.

'I think the first engine I fired on was with a driver called Tommy Pilkington and his fireman on a C13 tank engine. I just got up there with them – all unofficially – and had a go. I often did three or four hours extra for no pay.'

Harry seems to be able to pluck precise memories from the air – names of drivers, location of incidents, names of locomotives. His favourite engine was the Green Arrow, although he also fired on the *Flying Scotsman*.

'I certainly did,' he recalls, 'but it was tatty and run down then, not pristine like it is now. But the Green Arrow is the one I really remember. The 1936 Green Arrow was a wonderfully versatile engine, built originally for fully fitted freight, and its motto in those early days was "Guaranteed delivery next day". I remember one Green Arrow was called *St Peter's School*, but most didn't have names. The Green Arrow only had a six-wheel tender with a water capacity of 4,000 gallons and coal capacity of 7 or 8 tons, but she gave you an absolutely lovely ride and she steamed beautifully, which wasn't by any means true of all the old engines.'

Other engines Harry remembers with enormous affection are the D9s and the Tiny: 'Now that was just a simple little engine, but perfect in its way.'

When Harry was firing all the time, he would go through exactly the same routine every time he started his shift on the footplate. It was a self-imposed discipline that stood him in good stead.

'I'd always look at the boiler gauge glass first, because if the engine was in steam and you found you had no water you had to be quick and get some or there was a danger you'd drop your plug. That meant the lead plug in the bottom of the copper firebox, which protected the firebox. If there was no water, ultimately the lead plug would melt and the fire would drop out of the box through the hole before the copper box was ruined. But dropping a plug was about the worst thing you could do. Everyone would know about it and you'd never live it down. So after you'd looked at your gauge, and assuming it was all right, you'd check your fire. On allocation of your loco you'd have forty-five minutes to an hour preparation time, dependent on the class of loco. The larger-grate-area locos were allowed an hour.

'Building up a fire was an art in itself – you wanted to do it gently so as not to produce too much smoke. You didn't want the engine "blowing off" as we used to say –

that is you didn't want too much pressure before you were due to leave. On the C13s if you reached about 160lb and you weren't working it would blow off, but we'd normally leave the shed at about 140–160lb. Opening the dampers was one way to improve your fire, but there were other things you could do and things you needed to check.

'You had to know lots of little details – like the fact that the engine won't steam (that is, won't work properly) if the smokebox door is not sealed, because it will create a vacuum.'

Early turns at firing before he became a passed cleaner meant cadging a place on the footplate alongside older men who were keen to have an enthusiastic youngster on board; a youngster who would learn something but at the same time ease the burden of what was, at the best of times, very hard work.

'When I first used to go firing with Tommy Pilkington, I was really just helping because I was new to it. Keen as I was, I didn't know as much as Tommy's regular fireman. I didn't do it all, but it meant I got some practice and Tommy's fireman got a bit of a rest. The first thing you knew about firing was that it was very hard work and that the amount of shovelling – the rate at which you'd have to be adding coal to the fire – depended on the load.'

Harry remembers one interesting development when the footplate inspector George Slight at Newton Heath brought in what was called controlled firing. Instead of just judging how much coal to add to his fire, the fireman put on one round of coal every two minutes and stuck rigidly to that rate. The system was said to save a lot of coal and be just as efficient as firing to no obvious pattern.

'I remember we used an egg timer to tell when the two minutes was up,' says Harry with a grin. 'When the sand had gone through you put on another shovelful and turned your egg timer over again. You then stood back and waited till it was time for another shovelful.'

Like most firemen Harry is an expert on different types of coal – some he swears *by*, some he is more inclined to swear *at*!

'Of course, the best firing depends on having good coal. With good coal the art was always little and often; not keeping great mounds of coal permanently banked up. A shovel of coal thrown on to coal that hasn't already burned means you lose steam, so too much was as bad as too little. I always tried to make what I called a bright, thin fire, but what was best did vary from engine to engine. Early locos had long, narrow fireboxes, but later ones like the Atlantics had a wide box. With a wide box you had a greater area so it followed that you'd generate more heat. Locos with a wide firebox also had a carrying wheel under the cab to take the extra weight.'

It's difficult to imagine Harry, at well over 6ft tall, standing comfortably on the footplate, but the physical fitness that has clearly stayed with him through his long life must be at least partly due to those arduous years with the coal shovel.

'As a general rule freight trains didn't get good coal – that was kept for the passenger trains, especially the expresses to King's Cross. Darlton Main was wonderful steam coal – Yorkshire Hard we called it, and it made a very clean

Driver and fireman on a 4-4-2 locomotive, circa 1905. Credit: National Railway Museum/Science & Society

fire. The worst coal I think was that from the Wigan area – awful stuff it was.

'Great Western engines were built to burn South Wales anthracite, which is excellent coal. They were specially engineered for it. Operationally the Great Western had a reputation for slackness, but they had great engines. We used to get cross when we were kept waiting for Great Western trains at Banbury in Oxfordshire. I remember once we were kept waiting for two hours to cross from up yard to down sidings to return to Woodford. It was ridiculous and all down to their bad working.'

Harry's exasperation reveals a genuine distinction between the Great Western and other regions. He explains how on the LNER and the LMS the signalmen received a train report, and as the trains worked to time the signalmen always knew where they were at any time so they could work to maximum efficiency and not cause hold-ups.

'It was the same on the Great Central,' says Harry. 'The man in the box always knew exactly what times the trains were running to and he'd know how many wagons were on each train, so he could work out if they would fit in a loop. But it was all different on the Great Western – there the signalman had to ask where the expresses were. He often hadn't a clue. He'd assume they were running to time, but as often as not they weren't. This meant losing time by leaving freight in a loop while they sorted out all the other trains.

'Once I was on the footplate at Neasden. I was on a B1 designed for mixed traffic and we were waiting to work back to Woodford. Now the B1 was a good engine – in trials held in 1948 it worked out best on use of coal and water. Anyway, we got on the footplate and we had fifty vans behind us so we had the vacuum brakes on – they were operated by steam – and we had three parts of a boiler full of water. But I was with a slightly nervy driver who said we'd better get to Northolt Junction sharpish or we'd be behind time. As it turned out we got stuck behind a Great Western unfitted freight train all the way back. In fact that whole trip turned into a disaster.

'I remember we were on a rising gradient going over the Chilterns. If the signals were all off you could shoot over the hill and through High Wycombe and just keep on going. We decided to get water at Princes Risborough, but my nervy driver just missed the water column in the dark – he went past it, so that was that. We then kept going till we got to Brackley and then finally Woodford. By the time we got there we were right down on our water – it was a close-run thing that we got there at all. But the art and science of locomotive driving meant that there were no certainties; people did run out of water now and then and the train would just have to stop at a water column.'

Then came the day when Harry was passed for firing. He was passed by Tom Adams, a man with wide-ranging interests who was said to know the rule book by heart.

'Tom was an interesting man – he eventually became Lord Mayor of Manchester – but I remember him best from the time he watched me at work on the footplate. He was meticulous and hugely experienced; if he passed you, you knew you were doing something right.'

Harry was still firing and based at Chester from 1938 until war was declared the following year. He thought about trying to join up, but discovered that railwaymen who volunteered were not entitled to have their jobs back at the end of the war. Men who were called up, on the other hand, *were* guaranteed their old jobs, so Harry waited for call-up papers which, in the event, never arrived. But he has a particularly poignant memory of the days leading up to the end of peace.

'I can remember the Friday before war was declared we took a GC Pom-Pom (a J11 Class 0-6-0 freight engine) to Skelton Junction turntable where we were to back onto a passenger special. It was a lovely sunny day, but we took that special to Liverpool to pick up evacuated children. I can see them vividly now: they all had gas masks, and they all looked so sad. They were taken to Chester.'

Then suddenly, with his career apparently in full swing, Harry was made redundant again. It was October 1939 and the news was completely unexpected; but all was not quite lost as he was immediately offered another job.

'I was sent with three junior passed cleaners to Birkenhead where we worked the engines on the docks. Most of the work was shunting freight. I remember we had Sentinel shunting engines and we had to take them across a main road now and then at a place where a policeman was permanently stationed to give you permission to cross. Those were incredibly busy days – everyone was fighting to get their wagons to the side of the ships. When the first bombs began to drop on the

docks we would jump off the footplate and hide behind piles of sandbags. We were issued with helmets and gas masks and we wore them during a raid – strange sort of uniform for a train driver, but Liverpool was a dangerous place to be as it was very heavily bombed.

'We used to work the cattle trains from Birkenhead to York every Sunday night. They were J39 0-6-0s, the biggest engine allowed on the dock road; shunting engines, of course, had a shorter wheelbase.'

In 1941 Harry applied for a job in Liverpool and got it. But in May that year, before he actually took up his new position, the Blitz hit Liverpool.

'We were bombed for twelve hours every night for a week. On the railways we just had to stay at work right through it because I suppose we were part of the war effort. We drove with tarpaulin sheets over the cabs so the German pilots wouldn't see the flare from the firebox.

'We used to work incredibly long shifts through the war. Once on a Saturday night in 1941 I was rostered to work the 8.30pm express from Liverpool to Manchester and then work the 10.55pm back again. Anyway, we worked up to Manchester, got on the table and turned ready to go back. We were on red alert and didn't get to Warrington until midnight. We'd given a few American servicemen a lift on the footplate but we had to drop them at Warrington. I noticed that suddenly everyone on the platform at Warrington had vanished. We sat waiting for the guard to give us right of way but nothing happened. After a while I wandered back to the signal box, and the signalman told me that we couldn't go on to Liverpool because the whole of the central station and the surrounding buildings had been destroyed by the raids that night.'

Next morning, with Liverpool still out of the question, Harry and his driver went to Brunswick Yard instead. That shift had lasted fifteen hours instead of eight! But it was like that right through the war because, despite the risks, the amount of traffic had increased enormously. For Harry the bombs put paid to the docks for a while and he stayed at Brunswick.

'At Brunswick I fired for a man called Dick Lewis. He was a right sourpuss but a wonderful engineman. Running in the blackout he could stop on a threepenny bit. I remember on a D9 once passing Risley: as we levelled out, Dick notched her up a bit by fetching her back – that's what we called it when you reduced the travel valves on the pistons. It made the engine work economically: the steam did the work. He did it perfectly. This lifted the safety valve even with the injector on. Perfect superheating.'

Towards the end of the war, as well as meeting his future wife, Harry came across a man who wanted to work at Brunswick. As Harry was keen to get back to Chester they did an exchange.

'I got into the passenger link at Chester in 1945. That was the top link. I used to fire for a chap called Dick Orton. He was a nice chap but a bit of a character and a bit of an ale can – he said to me once, "Never let your wife know what you earn."

Lampman changing the oil lamps which illuminated the lenses of semaphore signals, circa 1936. The lamps burned for eight days and were changed once a week. Credit: National Railway Museum/Science & Society

'We had N5s at Chester, not the C13s we should have had. There were fifty or sixty drivers at Chester but they were all very resistant to change or to trying anything new. For example, they were used to short-haul work, and didn't feel confident on longer runs.

'Early one morning, as we were going out on the Chester road (which is hilly and difficult), I thought, "This engine isn't steaming well at all". It was one of the non-superheated engines. I said to Dick Orton, who was driving, "Let's go back and get a fresh engine". He said we'd better stick to this one as the replacement might be worse! I remember thinking, "How could anything be worse than this!"'

Before continuing his story Harry goes to some lengths to explain that not all the engines at Chester were bad as this example: 'We had GN4-4-2 tanks – now they were lovely little engines. They ran like sewing machines, but the men at Chester were so conservative that they were really afraid of those GN tanks.

'Anyway, at Manchester Dick agreed that we should have a look to see what the problem was with our engine, so we looked at what was called the petticoat pipe – it was the bit that directed the blast up out of the engine. A lug had come off and the pipe was leaning at an angle. We would never be able to steam properly with it like that. However, with a bit of luck and a lot of effort, we just about struggled back to Delamere on 130lb of steam.

'Now I'd worked like hell to get that engine back to Delamere, and all Dick could do was to tell me to get more coal on the fire. I was so angry because he'd refused to take a fresh engine when he should have. Delamere to Chester is downhill, and all the hard work had been done. Well, *he* then got angry and threatened me with a spanner, but I was the bigger man so I took it off him. He reported me, but I told the inspector the engine should never have been on the road. I also told the inspector that I'd put in for a transfer and that's exactly what I did. I went to Woodford near Rugby when I saw a note on the noticeboard from someone at Woodford who wanted to come up to Chester.'

Harry arrived at Woodford in 1946 and stayed till 1951. It was here that he enjoyed some of his best years on the railway. There was passenger work, express freight and ordinary freight using lots of different engines: Green Arrows, K3s – for the fish trains from Grimsby to Banbury – and those much-loved Tinys, together with North Easterns.

At the mention of the North Eastern Harry's eyes light up.

'Now the North Easterns were interesting engines. They were three cylinder passenger engines with a cab roof made of wood covered with pitch! They leaked a bit, but they always rode very nicely.

'You have to remember that on the footplate of LNER locomotives the controls and various features would be in different places on different engines. By contrast Great Western locomotives had footplates that were standard: everything was always in the same place and of a standard design. Take the firehole door. On the Great Western the firehole door was oval-shaped, on Great Central engines it was oval-shaped, and on North Eastern engines it was square.'

After five or six years at Woodford Harry was due to become a passed fireman: passed, that is, for driving. Then came devastation.

'I was just coming up for driving when I began to notice that I was having difficulty seeing signals at distance. I went to the optician who said my eyes were not good enough and I needed glasses. In those days there were only two jobs you could do on the railway if you wore specs – ticket collecting or signalling. I'd always been interested in signalling so I thought I'd better do that, but it was a terrible blow as I'd never thought that I wouldn't be able to drive.'

After the initial shock Harry took the setback in his stride.

'I knew a bit about signalling as I'd always stopped to talk to different signalmen along the way – one used to teach me chess! – and I suppose I was always interested in the rules and regulations and in the other man's job. The loco men were always a bit toffee-nosed about other jobs on the railway, but all the jobs were really essential to each other. How could the driver do his job without the signalman, or without the platelayer? Anyway, I went to see the signalling inspector and told him about my eyes. My chance of being a driver was gone, but I applied for a transfer as glasses were all right for signalmen. Eventually I was accepted – I was delighted as by this time I had two kids, but it was extremely disappointing to be off the footplate.'

There was a vacancy for a signalman at the first station north of Woodford, so Harry went down from Woodford every day to the signalling school at Nottingham.

'The instructor there was a marvellous chap and we got on very well. I was trained for six weeks Saturdays only. I was sent to a signal box at Charwelton in Oxfordshire to watch a signalman at work and learn the bell codes. We had an up and a down line, a refuge siding, goods yard and a little branch line to an iron ore mine, and a passenger loop on the up line.

'Charwelton was the signal box near the Catesby Tunnel which runs for 3,000 yards. The regulations here were stricter than they would normally have been – because of the tunnel – and one hour into my first day in the box there was an emergency. The emergency bell went and we discovered that the down freight had dropped a door. It gave me a fright, but the experience taught me a lot by having to deal with a crisis so early in my time.

'Working in the signal box was a lonely life in some ways, but we had old omnibus phones and we used to talk to each other – the signalmen, I mean. On the Rugby to Woodford line there were seven boxes and it was a very busy line for freight. There was seldom what we called a clear block – that is, a time when no trains were moving.

'I worked all the boxes from Charwelton (a class 4 box) to Woodford 1, then to Woodford 3 (a class 2 box). Class 1 was the busiest, class 5 the least busy.'

For many men whose hearts had been set on driving the move to the signal box could have been a blow from which it would have been difficult to recover, but for Harry it had its compensations. It was a place of quiet routine, but that routine was occasionally interrupted by moments of drama and even danger. The job of signalman was also one of enormous responsibility.

'Yes, there were occasional dramas – apart from the odd horse getting loose and stopping all the trains! I can remember one occasion at 2 o'clock in the morning – when, as you can imagine, it was normally as quiet as the grave – I heard footsteps on the steps outside the box. It gave me a fright, but it was only a soldier looking for a ride. I told him to go to Woodford and catch the night mail.'

From 1950 to 1955 Harry worked the various boxes. The signals inspector at the time was a Mr Darnell, and the two men became friends.

'I used to talk to him a lot, and after I did a correspondence course for signalmen and got a first-class pass, Darnell asked me if I'd thought about going into control. I hadn't, but I began to think about it then. By this time I'd moved to what was called special-class relief – this covered all the boxes at Woodford – but I said I'd try for a job at Rugby control. I went to Leicester to take the exam and passed.'

Harry became assistant controller at Rugby. His job was to collect up all the tickets for freight trains from Camden or wherever. The ticket would give details of the time the crew got on, the number of the locomotive, the load, and anything special or unusual. He would then pass the tickets to the controller. Harry dealt with Willesden in North London, Stoke, Birmingham and Crewe, but by 1956 the chance to get back to the running side of things proved too great a temptation.

'A pal of mine had gone from Rugby control up to Holyhead and he encouraged me to get back into running locos. I applied, did well in the interview, and ended up as running shift foreman at a place called Patricroft at Eccles in Lancashire. I was really an engine arranger, if you like. I had to make sure we had engines for all the different jobs we had to do; I helped provide the power and the crews for what we used to call "all traffic requirements". Everything had to go up on the train arrangements board on the wall or it wouldn't happen. This was 1956 and I was a class 2 supervisor. By 1959 I'd reached class 1, and rather than mustering the engines I was mustering the men.

'Another unusual incident I can recall was when I discovered a series of thefts. Quite by chance one morning I spotted a steam raiser who should have been off duty some two hours earlier. When I investigated I found crates of whisky in his cabin. The police were called and they discovered an organized gang was at work. Nine staff were sacked in the finish, they appeared in court, and I had to go along as a witness. I felt very sad about the whole thing, but they were foolish and they paid the price.'

This was about the time that diesels were coming in, but it wasn't until 1968 that steam finally disappeared.

'The steam chaps in the main were good at converting to diesel, but it must have been hard for them. A big difference between steam and diesel in my experience was that once you'd passed on steam you could drive all the steam engines. On diesel you had to pass on each different engine.'

By 1964 Harry was a senior supervisor at Newton Heath, and here he stayed for twenty years until his retirement in 1984.

'I enjoyed every bit of my career, and still wouldn't swap it for anything else: but the best part of it was steam working and signalling. I did a total of forty-nine years and three months – not bad really. I only remember one serious accident – I was firing for Dick Horton and we were on a passenger train from Manchester to Chester. We'd just left Cuddington to climb to Delamere. Coming round a bend and starting to climb I suddenly saw a brake van up ahead. The guard was on the floor but he hadn't put detonators down on the track to warn us. I slammed the brake on and shut the regulator off – we were working a C13 tank engine – but we hit that coal train hard. All I remember was that the impact threw coal all over me – I was buried in the stuff! It was like hitting a solid wall of rock because the train was full and it was so heavy it didn't give at all. The signalman had got on his bike and raced along the track to

try to stop us, but he was too late. The engine and the first five coaches were damaged, but not derailed. There was never an enquiry, but it looked to me like there had been a problem with the signals. Anyway, we were relieved by the recovery teams and we went home, but I was a bit nervy when working after dark for quite a while afterwards. The guard I'd spotted just before the impact was hurt slightly, but there were no other injuries which was lucky, but it was odd because no one ever asked if we were OK.

'One of the biggest changes I recall was that before about 1968 all the people who dealt with train crews had experience of steam; after that those in charge seemed to know nothing about it. The old steam boys seemed to vanish almost overnight.

'You had to know how to run a diesel engine from a technical point of view – if the earth link dropped, for example, you just stopped – and there was definitely more to go wrong than there had ever been on steam, but steam took skill and experience. You had to build up your power; with diesel it was there ready for you.

'The truth is that people loved working steam *and* diesel – you had to be an enthusiast to work on the railways then. Of course there were practices that would be frowned on now – footplate men drank the odd pint during working hours, for example, but of course there were always two people on the footplate so they could help each other and make sure everything ran smoothly. Single manning, which is what you had on diesel, was a real shock for some of the old boys.

'But when I was a signalman, single-line working gave me some of the most interesting experiences because occasionally I had to act as a pilotman. On one occasion I was in charge of single-line working between Staverton and Charwelton. I had to put the system into operation on the first available train, which happened to be a passenger train called the Farnborough Flyer. I was at Staverton Road waiting for this train and when it arrived I had to ride on the footplate of the leading loco. I should add that this train was double-headed – in other words, pulled by two locos. Anyway, I got up on the footplate and there was my old friend George Tasker. He was delighted to see me, but in a foul mood because I was causing his train to be delayed. He was the footplate inspector in charge.

'To put single-line working into operation I'd had to issue the signalman with special forms which had to be countersigned by me. I also had to show myself to all the staff working on the track, for no movement could take place without my being there to see it. All these precautions show just how careful we were about safety in those days.'

Down Lambeth way

They were taking on new van boys at the goods depot, and among the applicants was a smart little Cockney lad. 'What's your name?' asked the clerk. ''Arry Coggins, sir.' 'Where do you live?' came the next query. 'Lambeth, sir.' 'Lambeth, eh? Have you lived there all your life?' 'No, not yet, sir' came the prompt retort.
Our Best Railway Stories, 1900

The Brighton train

'This ticket,' said the ticket collector to the festive passenger at Victoria station, 'is for Margate, but this is the Brighton train.' 'Strewth,' ejaculated the merry one, 'hadn't you bedder put the engine-driver right at once?'
Our Best Railway Stories, 1900

Going uphill

Let those who are sceptical as to the practicability of constructing a railway *to profit* over a hilly country, without encountering the enormous cost of securing what are called easy gradients, visit the Hartlepool Railway, where they will find a locomotive engine with its tender pulling a train of three or four passenger carriages up a short inclined plane of 1 in 30 and two long inclined planes of 1 in 35, at velocities of from 20 to 25 miles per hour, four times in the day; and the only obstacle to its

ascent (with still greater weights) appears to arise from the slipping of the wheels, or their want of adhesion to the rails in wet weather. This engine is furnished with 14in cylinders and six 4½ft wheels coupled together.

Who, then, shall venture to assert that railways will not hereafter be laid over the rough surface of any country hitherto deemed inaccessible by them? If the tread or tire of the wheels of such a locomotive were considerably widened, and the main rails upon such inclined planes laid upon longitudinal sleepers and an extra rail of wood or rough – why not cogged iron? – fixed outside the main rail, to which the tire of the engine (but not the carriages) wheels should extend, their adhesive power, we imagine, might be doubled.
Durham Advertiser, 1870

Stock by rail

During the past month vast numbers of sheep have been slaughtered by the Darlington butchers, and have been sent by railway to London. The butter wives frequenting Barnard Castle market were not a little surprised on Wednesday se'nnight to discover that, through the facilities offered by the railways, a London dealer had been induced to buy butter in their market for the supply of the cockneys, and in consequence the price went up 2d per pound immediately. This rise, however, did not deter the agent from purchasing, and 2,000 pounds of butter were quickly bought, sold, and packed off for the great Metropolis, where it would again be exhibited, and sold to the London retailers by five o'clock on Friday morning.

At a meeting of the Statistical Society a paper was read on the agricultural prices of the parishes of Middlesex. The writer proceeded to say that the railway had greatly affected prices in the cattle market at Southall, and had occasioned much discontent among the farmers,

who complained that, in consequence of the facility that it afforded for the rapid transfer of stock from one county to another, they had been deprived of the advantages which they formerly possessed from their proximity to London. Five hundred head of sheep and 100 head of cattle had upon more than one occasion been suddenly introduced into the market from the West of England, and prices had been proportionately forced down.

But, as a rule, on the great through lines, in 1843, every thing except passenger traffic was a very secondary affair. The Great Western was earning £13,000 a week from passengers and only £3,000 from goods
Great Northern Advertiser, November 1843

Empress brought to a halt

On the occasion of one of the return journeys from Holyhead I arranged in order to give the empress the opportunity of enjoying one of the prettiest views in North Wales, to stop the train near Llanfair, shortly before reaching the Britannia Tubular Bridge, at a well known point from whence the charming scene of the Menai Straits, the Telford Bridge and the Snowdon range of mountains were all obtainable and with which she was much pleased. But before reaching the appointed spot the train had been unexpectedly brought to a stand through the electric communication ringing in the vans, indicating that something was wrong.

The train was stopped in accordance with rule but no one made any signs of help being required; the department from which the signal had been given was easily discovered and we found that in total ignorance of the English notice that the handle was to be pulled only in case of emergency, one of the Austrian footmen had hung his great coat on this convenient peg and innocently caused the signal of danger to be given.
The Railways of England, W. M. Acworth, 1889

Infernal railway

On the completion of the viaduct, one of the patent six-wheel, long boiler locomotives, constructed by Robert Stephenson and Co, which had been sent by sea to the spot, and put together on the line, was slowly driven over the novel structure. The passage was a new kind of exploration. The accuracy and finish of the timberwork and plate-laying was thus, for the first time, tested, and the section of the tunnel, which varied from length to length, was examined by means of the passage of a wooden frame, which gave a clearance of six inches beyond the most prominent angles of any of the carriages, the top of the horse-boxes being one of the most awkward projections.

The slow passage that was dictated by prudence was enveloped in a cloud of steam, which from time to time blinded driver, stoker, and engineer. At other times the glare from the open firebox, on the reflecting surface of the vapour, gave a strangely infernal lustre to the exploring party. It was well that they went slowly. Halfway through the tunnel, the funnel of the locomotive came in contact with a piece of brickwork. It was necessary to unscrew the funnel, to lean it to one side until the obstacle was passed, and to make the necessary corrections in all parts before the return trip.

It was to ensure the safety of the passengers through this Stygian pass, where a head too curiously thrust out of a carriage window might have come into fatal collision with the wall of the tunnel, that the expedient was adopted of fixing brass bars outside the windows, a provision intended to be temporary, but which has been adopted to the permanent discomfort of the passengers on certain Kentish lines of railway.
The Railways of England, W. M. Acworth, 1889

Credit: National Railway Museum/Science & Society

THE
FLYING SCOTSMAN
1862 – 1962

PUBLISHED BY BRITISH RAILWAYS (EASTERN REGION) (PP.5038)　　　PRINTED IN GREAT BRITAIN　　　WATERLOW & SONS LIMITED LONDON AND DUNSTABLE

No smoking

Passengers who endeavoured to solace themselves on their journey with tobacco met with scant sympathy. Here is one notice: 'A young barrister on the Northern Circuit, a Mr Hay, was recently fined 20 shillings by the county magistrates at the Moot Hall, Newcastle, for smoking cigars in one of the coaches of the Newcastle & North Shields Railway Company on the preceding day.'

It is, adds the editor, 'that the public should know that there is power under the Act of Parliament to punish persons who offend against good taste and propriety by smoking in railway carriages whether closed or open.'

A foreign gentleman, writes a correspondent of the *Mechanics' Magazine,* in September, 1842, was smoking a cigar in a train coming from Brighton to London. The guard warned him that the practice was not allowed. Nevertheless the gentleman continued to smoke, and finished his cigar. At the next station he was met by a demand for his ticket, ordered out of the carriage and the guard, addressing one of the officers on the platform, warned him that 'that person was not to be allowed to proceed to London by any train that night – and there the gentleman was left'.

The passenger (so says the *Railway Times,* which repeats the story) 'suffered most properly for persisting in violating the laws of the Company'.

Even this can hardly match in occurrence what happened some years later on the Edinburgh and Glasgow line. A gentleman, well known at the time in the west of Scotland, was in a train going to Edinburgh. He smelt tobacco, and, calling the guard, complained that someone was smoking in the train. The guard failed, or said he failed, to find the offender, and the offensive smell continued to annoy the old gentleman. He therefore brought an action against the Company for the inconvenience to which he had been subjected, and recovered £8 6s 8d (£100 Scots) as damages in the Court of Session.

Railway Reminiscences, G. P. Neele, 1904

Rigid discipline

It is not difficult to find evidence that in the early days the railway companies were able to treat their passengers with a rigour of discipline that would be impossible in these days of keen competition for public favour. The London & Birmingham, had, we read, upwards of 200 men, wearing a peculiar distinguishing costume, sworn in as special constables to enforce a proper attention to the rules of the establishment. Considering that guards and porters together only numbered 190, this seems a large number, even allowing for the fact that they were signalmen as well. But then the rules were both multifarious and stringent.

Lapdogs, for which the minimum charge was 10 shillings, were apt to be smuggled. People would insist on coming to see their friends off on the platform, and this was strictly forbidden on the Great Western and elsewhere. A passenger, instead of walking along the train and looking for a seat,

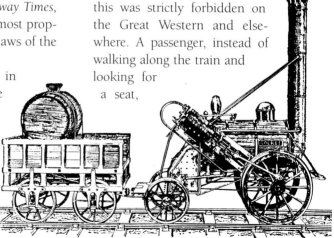

had a fixed and numbered place assigned him at the booking office. A correspondent of *The Times* writes that, having arrived at Paddington four minutes before the time advertised for the starting of a first-class train, he was refused admission and obliged to return home, a distance of 5 miles, besides delaying an important business for two days.

Another tells the same story from Brighton, with the additional aggravation that the officials acknowledged that he really would have been in time only that their clocks were wrong.
The Railways of England, W. M. Acworth, 1889

German efficiency

On the railway from Vienna to Baden no tickets are given out within the quarter of an hour preceding the starting of the train. We presented ourselves at the office at Baden half an hour previous. It had begun to rain heavily, and the crowds of disappointed pleasure-seekers stood at the window waiting for tickets.

Only one man delivered them; and he, with most ominous coolness, every few minutes turned his eye on the office clock. At the moment the finger reached the quarter he stopped, declared the time up, and refused to deliver another ticket. It was in vain that the indignant throng declared that they had already, many of them, been waiting

half an hour: he only answered that was the rule, he did not make it; and the poor people must wait, not only the quarter till this train went, but another hour or two for the next. The quarter passed, and the train set out not half filled, leaving the wretched crowd in the rain! Never was the beauty of German formality so beautifully carried out.
Rural and Domestic Life in Germany, William Howitt, 1842

Coachman's answer

The coachmen heard the tidings of the approach of their ruthless iron rivals with feelings that passed through the stages of incredulous contempt, of uneasy curiosity, and of alarmed enmity. When a Hertfordshire Vicar threatened the proprietor of 'the coach' which so often brought him from his Saturday night's whist parties to his Sunday morning's duties, with iron roads and steam coaches, Mr Wyatt, the coachman, coolly replied: 'And do you know what I hears people a-talking of? They means to send down here a patent cast-iron parson, to go by steam, and then they says they allas know where to find him.'
The History of the English Railway, J. Francis, 1851

Where's the navvy?

Even unlimited beer at times palls on the taste. Men with a few shillings in their pockets are often disposed to seek amusements for the most part only readily to be found in great towns. While not given to dancing like his Continental neighbours, the well-paid English labourer is not proof at all times against a weakness for female society, even if not of the most unexceptionable decorum. Thus, after a pay, some of the most hard-working, and, therefore, richest navvies might wander off to the nearest cities. They might not return, and then their places would have to be supplied from the ever-circulating stream of inquirers for employment, that always fringes the course of large public works.

Gangers (that is, foremen) always like to keep their best hands and will prefer receiving a repentant and penniless navvy, on his return from what they call being 'off on the randy', to taking on a stranger.
Railway Reminiscences, G. P. Neele, 1904

Guilty of neglect

It is impossible to avoid taking comfort at times from the admitted weaknesses of great men. A writer was accompanying Mr Brunel over a portion of the South Wales Railway. They passed through the little town of Kidwelly, where the sturdy round tower of the castle still recalls the aspect of feudal times.

'Do you know,' said the great Engineer, 'I always feel very sneaking when I pass this place. When we first obtained the Bill for the line, the good people here were overjoyed. They held a public meeting, and resolved to present me with the freedom of the town. It was drawn out in form, and sent me with a letter from the mayor, and, in fact, in a gold-plated box. Of course I felt gratified, and I waited a day or two before acknowledging the letter, as I was extremely busy, and I wished to do so in suitable terms. So a week or two slipped by and I thought that I must make my apologies in person. But from that time to this the opportunity has not presented itself. I am ashamed to say that I have never even thanked them, and I feel as if I must rush through the town whenever I have to pass it, from being unable to excuse my neglect.'
Personal Recollections of English Engineers, F. R. Conder, 1868

Brunel in search of a pint

The Quaker Director gave a great breakfast to celebrate the opening of one of the lines with which Mr Brunel was connected. Everything was there that could be wished for, or thought of, with the sole but important exception of wine. Champagne was an abomination to the Friends. The Director was a severe teetotaller. He was not even content to throw the onus on the conscience of his guests, as was once done by the no less plain-spoken lady who presided over a dinner table at Birmingham. 'There is wine on the sideboard,' she remarked during an ugly pause: 'We think it sinful to drink it; but it is here for those who have not thought it essential to abstain.'

But Brunel could not make a breakfast on pines, grapes, and coffee. He asked for a pint of beer. The host was inexorable.

'I cannot breakfast at this hour without something of the kind,' said Brunel. 'I must help myself, and return to finish your good things.'

Followed by two or three of the party, he left the Quaker's banquet, and, entering a public-house hard by, enjoyed a good draught of ale, returning contented and in perfect good temper to his intolerant entertainer.
The Railways of England, W. M. Acworth, 1889

Pay dispute

The county magnates looked with disfavour on the railway. The main occupation of the Pembrokeshire landlords was fox hunting. How could the hounds be expected to keep the scent if people were allowed to make great ditches 20ft deep, and corresponding banks across the countryside? The invasion was intolerable.

Then as to wages. It was actually stated that the railway contractors had the extravagance to pay half-a-crown a day. Eighteen

pence a day was fair agricultural remuneration. The Welsh labourer did not ask more and if he should do so he would not get it.

It was immoral in the highest degree that English engineers should come down to disturb this satisfactory state of things and to make the country people discontented.
Personal Recollections of English Engineers,
F. R. Conder, 1868

The engineers' bet

The unpleasant feeling between the Engineer of the London & Birmingham, and the Engineer of the Grand Junction Railway (lines quite as much functions of one another as were the Paris & Rouen, and Rouen & Havre), was subsequently removed. Mr Locke came down to Chester, on the occasion of the inquest into the Dee Bridge accident, to support Mr Stephenson. A little incident at a somewhat later date showed the pleasant relations of the two men, both with each other, and with their frequent opponent, Brunel. The three were travelling together in a railway carriage; Stephenson wrapped in a dark plaid, on the exact disposition of the folds of which he somewhat prided himself.

He saw Brunel regarding him with a curious eye. 'You are looking at my plaid, ' said he.

'I'll bet you ten pounds that you cannot put it on properly at the first time.'

'Very well,' said the other, 'I have no objection to bet ten pounds. But I won't take your money. I bet ten pounds against the plaid. If I put it on right when we get out on

LMS **THE PERMANENT WAY**
RELAYING
by Stanhope Forbes R.A.

Credit: National Railway Museum/Science & Society

the first platform, it is mine. If I miss, I pay you ten pounds.'

'Done,' said Stephenson, and resumed his conversation with Locke. But Brunel sat in a brown study, and said not a word till they arrived at the next station.

'Now then, Stephenson, give me the plaid to try,' said he, as he stepped on the platform. Robert Stephenson slowly unwound the garment. Brunel promptly wound it around his own shoulders, with as much composure as if he had pulled on a great coat.

'It is a first attempt,' said he, 'but I think the plaid is mine.' For many a day did he rejoice in its comfort.

'But had you never tried before?' said a friend. 'No,' said Brunel, 'but when Stephenson challenged me, I was not going to give up; so I began immediately to study the folds, and to make out how he had put it on. I got the thing pretty clear in my head before we got to the station, and when I saw him get out of it I knew that I was right, so I put it on at once.' A playful instance of the concentrated meditation Mr Brunel gave to any subject on which he fixed his thoughts.
Personal Recollections of English Engineers, F. R. Conder, 1868

Irish works

'Ye need be under no alarm in coming among us,' said the manager of a branch of the Bank of England to an English engineer, on his arrival to commence some considerable works in the South of Ireland. 'If ye don't meddle with land, and don't interfere with labour, no one will shoot ye, unless it's quite by mistake.'

'As we cannot make railways without taking possession of land, and the employment of labour, yours is a particularly reassuring welcome,' was the reply. It may be mentioned by the way, that the bank in question had the advantage of keeping its own beggar, a tall lame man with a big stick, who always stood inside the outer door of the establishment, and begged regularly of the customers.
Railway Reminiscences, G. P. Neele, 1904

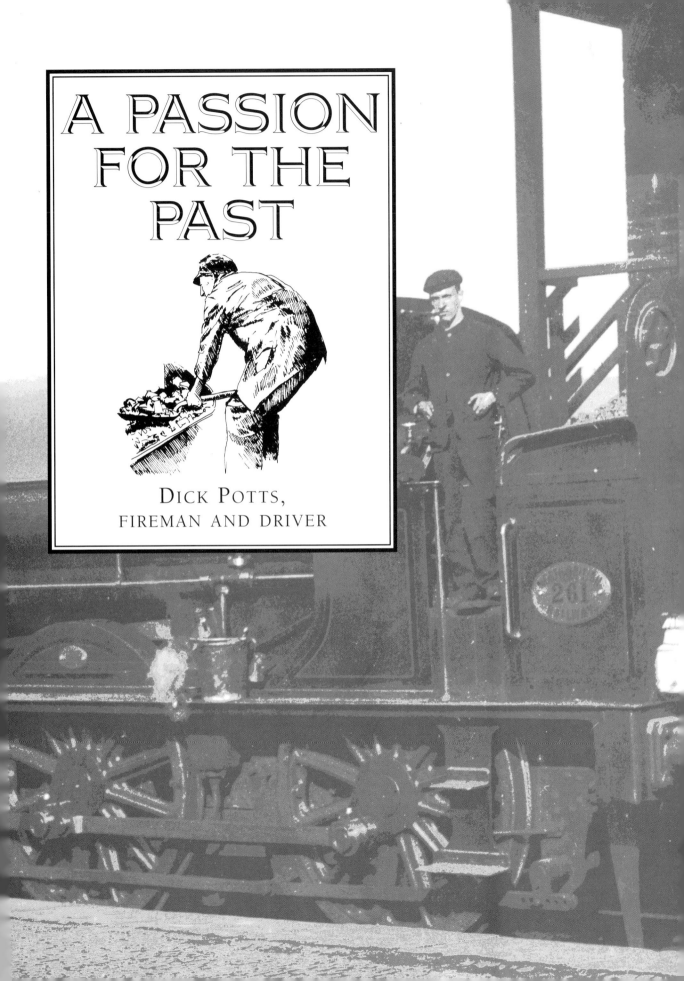

A PASSION FOR THE PAST

Dick Potts,
FIREMAN AND DRIVER

Painter, historian, archivist and railwayman, Dick Potts has devoted his life to locomotives and the men who worked them. His home in Birmingham is just a few hundred yards from the old Tyseley engine shed – now a museum – where he, his father and his grandfather spent their working lives. Today in retirement Dick is slowly building up a picture of the lives of all the men who worked in the Tyseley shed over the ninety-odd years it remained in use.

But how did it all start? Well, as Dick explains, it was a combination of family tradition and individual enthusiasm.

'I was born in a house overlooking the main line at Small Heath here in Birmingham. We lived in Byron Road – which has almost all been demolished now – and my dad was a driver. He'd started as a cleaner at Kidderminster in 1917 on the Great Western. When he was made a fireman he moved to Small Heath where my mother lived with her mother. My grandmother took in lodgers – mostly railwaymen – and that's how my mum and dad met. Dad was my grandmother's lodger!

'When mum and dad got married they stayed on in the house, and one of my earliest memories is of my mum standing at the bottom of the garden watching the trains go by. She used to remember all their names, too.'

Dick was born in 1929. By the time he was five his parents had moved, but not far; they were still in Small Heath, and his father still set off each morning on the long walk to the Tyseley shed.

'I must have been about five because although I can't remember much from that time, I can just about recall the trams clanking up and down the road, and by the time I was six they'd been replaced by trolleybuses. Each morning my dad used to walk along the railway track for half an hour to get to work. It seems amazing now, but he did that every day from 1917 until he retired in 1965 – almost fifty years.'

Despite both Dick's father and grandfather being drivers there was little talk about life at work. Railway work was just hard and badly paid in those days, and in the evenings Dick's father had better things to think about.

'Dad wasn't much of a talker, so I found out very little about what life was like on

Fireman Potts and driver Timmis in 1957

the railways in his younger days. I know it was unusual on the Great Western to stay so long in one place – by the time I was thinking of leaving school dad had been at Tyseley for twenty-five years. Normally on the Great Western they told footplate staff to move for promotion, and you didn't argue. I suppose my dad was just lucky. My grandfather, Edward Turner, my mother's father, started at Neath in South Wales in 1877. He moved to Westbourne Park in London, in 1891, just before the last broad gauge trains worked from there. Three moves later, in 1901, he was at Bordesley, and when it was closed in 1908 all the staff moved to the new depot at Tyseley. Unfortunately I never met him as he died in 1915, hence the need for my grandmother to take in lodgers.'

Dick is something of an expert on the early railway, and his sitting-room walls are lined with books and records. He takes a particular interest in Brunel's broad gauge system. No broad gauge engines have survived, but at Steam, the museum in Swindon, a replica exists for which parts of the original *North Star* – a nineteenth-century broad gauge engine – were used. A working replica is on view and in steam occasionally at the National Railway Museum at York.

'Steam engines built in the 1920s, '30s and '40s were bigger than the old broad gauge engines,' says Dick, 'but by the standards of the day – and we're talking about the mid-Victorian period – broad gauge engines would have seemed extraordinary. You have to remember that the narrow gauge – still in use now – is just 4ft 8½in wide. The old broad gauge distance between the wheels was an incredible 7ft ¼in, so the engines had to be correspondingly huge.'

Dick's enthusiasm for the railway past reveals itself in the detailed paintings he works on in retirement. He started painting in about 1955, self-taught initially, but improved after spending holidays at the St Ives School of Painting during the 1970s and 1980s. He has completed several hundred pictures, but has a particular fondness for portraying the history of the railway and particularly the old broad gauge engines.

'Broad gauge was Brunel's great idea. It wasn't a huge problem in the early days,' he explains, 'because although the original narrow gauge also ran from the 1830s there weren't that many miles of track anyway, broad or narrow. Problems arose when the mileage started to increase rapidly every year. Where Brunel's Great Western broad gauge met other areas that used narrow gauge – at Gloucester, for example – you had problems, and these got worse as the system expanded.

'Where the two systems met, everything had to be transferred from one train to another to continue the journey. But narrow gauge was always going to win in the end because by the time the matter was thrashed out in parliament – it was called the Battle of the Gauges – there was already more narrow gauge mileage laid down. That said, many businessmen and others still supported Brunel's 7ft gauge. Broad gauge was never banned, but parliament eventually agreed that wherever broad gauge existed any new track had to be mixed – in other words the tracks for broad gauge had to have narrow gauge rails built within them. Imagine the problems that caused where you had points!'

Dick's knowledge of this and other aspects of railway history appears inexhaustible, and he is a meticulous chronicler of railway facts and figures. However, his own career on the railways almost came unstuck at the outset. Unlike many railwaymen, Dick's father had no intention of allowing his son to continue the family tradition.

'Right from my earliest days I wanted to be an engine driver, but when my dad

4056 Princess Margaret *at Swindon Works, 1956*

and mum looked at what I might do when I left school they decided – like a lot of parents at the time – that they wanted something better for their children. This was understandable because in the 1920s and '30s conditions on the railway were grim. The steam engines offered the footplate men very little protection from the elements, and the wages were appalling.

'Friends of my dad's who worked in factories were always telling him he could earn a lot more elsewhere. He didn't move, but when it came to my turn to get a job dad said he wouldn't have me on the railway. I suppose this was also partly down to the fact that if I'd made a mess of things people would have come to him and said, "Oh your lad's mucked up again", and he didn't want that. And he really did think I'd have a better life elsewhere.'

So at the age of just fourteen Dick left school and started work as a telegraph boy in the post office. He was one of that vast number of young men who walked and biked around the country delivering this now-vanished form of communication.

'Every morning I'd join dozens of other boys all employed to do the same thing. Telegrams have disappeared now, but they were short messages on tape that was stuck down on paper. They were tapped out by an operator at one telegraph office and instantly received at another office, which might be at the other end of the country. They were expensive to send, and of course you had to have one army of people typing the messages and another army receiving them. Then you needed the boys to get on their bikes and take the messages round to houses, offices and factories.'

Telegrams weren't just delivered to people's houses when there was an emergency. Offices, factories and other big businesses routinely used them so there was a lot of traffic. The telegraph boys had little pill-box hats, a leather pouch for the telegrams and, as Dick explains with a smile, an incredibly heavy cast-iron bicycle. The telegrams themselves were always delivered in yellow envelopes.

'We worked shifts, but at fourteen I wasn't allowed to do really long hours. I was a telegraph boy for two years and by the end of it I reckon I knew every street in Birmingham!'

In 1945 Dick passed the Civil Service exams and embarked on the next stage of his career. He became an SC&T: a sorting clerk and telegraphist. He learned to type on a teleprinter in just one month.

'Right from the word go we had to type with a screen over the keys so we couldn't see them. Endlessly typing As then Bs was very boring but it made you learn. The GPO wanted accuracy, not speed. Once I was trained I went into a room with hundreds of other telegraphists, and I found the work mind-destroying because you couldn't even see what you were typing – that came out on tape somewhere on the other side of the country. Some of the girls who'd done the work for years were absolutely brilliant – they could type the messages with perfect accuracy while reading a book at the same time.

'Just to give you an idea of the volume of work – the telegrams for the Dublin section had four people working full time twenty-four hours a day, seven days a week, just sending money orders!'

Two more years passed and then, like so many eighteen-year-olds, Dick was called up for national service into the RAF.

'The first fortnight – the square-bashing fortnight I suppose you'd call it – was awful, but then they discovered I was GPO-trained so I was sent to a place called Chicksands in Bedfordshire to the Central Signals Station for the RAF. It was hidden in a forest so you couldn't see it from the air. I remember getting off the bus from Bedford in pitch darkness and then trying to spot the tiny red light at the top of the transmitter in the middle of the forest. You'd then use that little light to guide you because of course there were no street lights. It was an odd place, though, because the top of the transmitter mast was roughly on a level with Bedford so you could see the red light more or less straight ahead of you. The camp itself – beneath the transmitter – was in a deep valley.

'For a year I tapped away at codes that meant absolutely nothing to me. After about nine or ten months the whole camp moved to Bletchley Park and the whole time I was there I never heard a word about code breaking – hadn't a clue it was happening, which shows how good their security was!'

But throughout these early years Dick maintained his fascination in the railways. If anything, not being allowed to work on the railway increased his determination to escape the drudgery of endless typing.

'While I was at Chicksands I used to go train-spotting at Hitchin whenever I had any free time. This would have been 1947 or early 1948. I loved it because coming from Birmingham I'd never seen LNER engines before and here they all were – Pacifics, A4s, all thundering up and down through the station. It was heaven. I used to sit watching them for hours, even in the dark when it was particularly exciting because a lot of those drivers used to thrash their engines, and you'd see sparks from the ashpans through the wheels and streams of fire from the chimneys.

'One day a railway policeman walked up to me and said, "I've seen you here every day and I've had reports about you writing things in a notebook". He was very suspicious, but when I explained what I was doing he was delighted. I'd met a fellow railway enthusiast. He told me to come as often as I liked and said he'd make sure no one bothered me in future.'

Dick's passion for detailed record-keeping – a passion that continues to this day –

started early. At eighteen it wasn't enough for him to *see* what was going on: he had to record it.

'I think even other train-spotters must have thought I really was mad,' he says with a grin, 'because I used to write absolutely everything down: the name of the engine, the number and the state of the engine, whether it looked clean or not. I've still got all my record books.

'On moving to Bletchley on the old LMS I did the same thing and I built up a huge record of engines. The only sad thing was that I couldn't take photographs – even if I could have afforded a camera it wouldn't have been allowed.

'But when I watched those drivers I thought, "I'm not going back to the post office: if they can drive then so can I". The only obstacle was my dad. And right enough he was a bit upset when I got home after demob and told him I'd decided to work on the railways, but to his credit he accepted it. He still didn't like the idea of me starting at Tyseley – because he was sensitive to criticism – so he told me to go to Saltley on the London Midland Region, but that was a bit like asking someone to change their political party!'

In the end Dick did start work at Tyseley, in December 1949. It was what he had always wanted and, despite his father's dire warnings that he would regret it, he loved every minute.

'I was just glad to be there: I think I was made for it. Several men who are my

Driver Timmis on the footplate, 1957

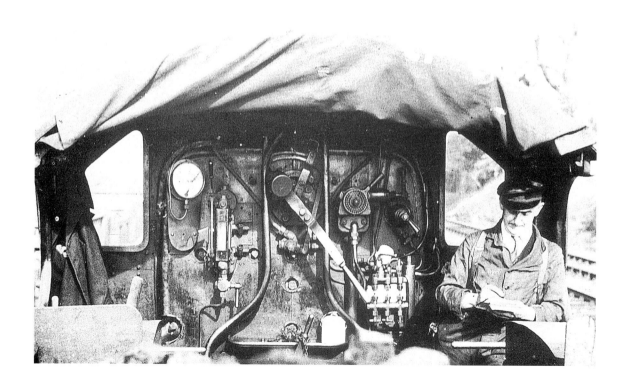

Fireman Potts at Didcot, 1957

friends to this day started with me. Like me they were barmy about trains, although I think I was the only train-spotter among them.'

Dick started as a cleaner and although, as he explains, everyone pretty much knows what an engine cleaner does, few people today realize quite what an arduous task it was.

'Everyone says it was dirty, but what they forget is that it was dirt like you've never seen dirt before! The truth is that even after a bath – or several baths – you couldn't get the dirt out. It would get so deep into your skin and under your nails that it seemed like it would be there forever. It also made you stink to high heaven. You carried the smell of soot with you wherever you went.'

But Dick was in his element. By this time he had acquired a camera and he began taking photographs of the engines after he and his mates had cleaned them, which now form part of his huge archive.

'Our enthusiasm for cleaning can be illustrated by an engine we did called *Marble Hall*. It had virtually no paint on it so it looked completely black, but because we wanted to make something – anything! – on it look good, we tried to outdo each other by polishing the copper work on the chimney, even though the whole of the "paintwork" was such a mess. On another occasion we had to clean the standby engine – *Wrottesley Hall* – for the Royal Train. She had a black safety valve cover and we scratched it to see if there was brass underneath the paint and dirt. There was, so we spent ages cleaning it up: we even went and bought our own emery paper! The gaffer said it looked wonderful and the fireman called us bloody fools, but he looked pleased all the same.'

For a short time Dick spent his shifts cycling round the streets near Tyseley in the early hours calling up the drivers, but he always preferred cleaning.

'I did labouring jobs at this time too because they were better paid than cleaning. How the permanent coal men did it I will never know. It was the toughest work you can imagine yet they made it look easy. All day they'd be shovelling coal out of huge trucks into smaller iron-wheeled wagons. Then they had to push these incredibly heavy wagons across the depot and tip them into a tender.

'When I worked with the labourers I couldn't keep up with them. They shovelled non-stop for maybe twelve hours. My hands were red raw after a couple of hours and my back would be killing me, but the full-time men would be swinging that shovel as if it was the easiest thing in the world. There was a bloke called Sailor who used to shovel the ashes out from under the engines, through a door in the side of an ash wagon standing alongside. As the wagon filled up he'd have to shut the side door and lift each shovelful high up over the top and into the wagon. Hour after hour he made it look easy and never even broke into a sweat. I remember watching him and thinking, "God all ruddy mighty!"

'There were huge numbers of men who spent their lives shovelling like this – the coal men and fire droppers and I had enormous admiration for them.'

But anything that took Dick away from the locomotives he loved was bound to be of less interest. Cleaning may have been grubby, but it gave him the most detailed knowledge of how an engine actually worked. But there were still occasions when getting the inside story meant going much further than one might like to imagine.

'When we cleaned the biggest fireboxes we used to climb inside them! They might be 10ft long on a really big engine. Working inside the firebox had to be thorough, and when you're young you don't worry so much about the safety angle. We'd be in there bent double and raking the ash down into the ashpan and brushing all the barnacles off the tubeplate. The dust and heat were incredible and you were always told by the boilersmith when you climbed out of a firebox that you should stay still in the cab for a few minutes while you cooled down otherwise you'd faint.

'We heard stories – and I'm pretty sure they were accurate – of men going into the firebox while the fire was still burning! I wonder what the health and safety people would have to say about that today.'

Dick was a cleaner for just six months. He moved on quickly because Birmingham, like so many areas, was very short of men. Many firemen who hadn't been allowed to pack the job in during the war because of the Works Act (which introduced restrictions on certain essential jobs) left as soon as they were no longer compelled to stay. They went into the factories where they could earn more money, but that meant rapid promotion for those who remained.

'In 1950 I went to Bordesley station as a passed cleaner. That was always the first move for a cleaner from Tyseley because at Bordesley it was all firing on shunting

engines – the first step for a fireman. It was hard work because it was busy – it was a shed that worked twenty-four hours a day, seven days a week, with no let-up. I fired there for six months and was never given a single instruction, no lessons, no exam. I just got up on the footplate and started shovelling. It was easier for me because I was so interested, but I think it would have been murder for anyone else.

'I first fired for a driver called Wally Woodman who was a miserable sod, but with some excuse as he was in poor health. I made a pig's ear of it, and although he was a bit grumpy Wally tried to help. My problem was that I couldn't raise enough steam. Next day I fired for a gent called Arthur Rogers, a wonderful bloke and, like me, a real railway enthusiast. We had a great time and in one day I began to get the hang of it. The following week I was with a driver called Dai Davies and I was with him for six months.

'Dai was famous for leaving his fireman to do all the work – and I really do mean *everything*. He'd sit down and relax while you fired and drove the engine, but I didn't mind because it gave me the chance to learn. Shunting can be very boring, but it's great if you're working with a mate. If your driver won't say a word to you, or help you, it's hell, and scores of firemen packed the job in because of it. Some went because the driver decided he didn't like them, or they were no good and the driver's word was law – if he said you were out then you were out.

'The worst place I can remember working with the shunters was at Hockley. Here we were moving box vans – rows of them in a tunnel – so you couldn't see a thing.'

After six months' shunting Dick moved back to Tyseley, but 'tripping' to different yards from Bordesley yard – he worked to Solihull, Hall Green and Handsworth, usually with a small shunting engine. But wherever you were shunting the skills required of the fireman were the same.

'When you were firing on a shunting engine you needed plenty of steam, particularly where you were moving wagons full of heavy freight like coal. The fire had to be thick enough to withstand the blast, and to give the driver plenty of steam when shunting long "rafts" of wagons backwards and forwards.

'Take an engine where, for example, the fire grate might be 5ft by 5ft with fire bars running across it 1in thick and kept apart by lugs. The firelighter would start the fire with a bit of waste – odd bits of rags and sticks and paraffin dropped in through the fire door off a shovel – or he might have a central brazier in the shed and he'd take shovelfuls of burning coal from it to each engine that had to be lit. At Tyseley there were braziers like this – we called them devils. He'd then go round the shed adding a little more to each fire on each circuit until each engine had a good fire going.

'When the fireman arrived he'd use a dart or a pricker – an iron rod – to lift and spread the fire around over the bars before adding more coal. He'd keep adding coal, picking the big lumps by hand first, and spreading the fire till he had a good depth.

'About 4 or 5in of fire spread evenly across the firebox would give you enough steam for pottering about, but for heavy shunting you might need a fire 4ft thick and spread to that depth right across the grate.

'On some engines it was best to have the fire deeper at the side and shallower in the middle of the grate or sloping down to the front. When the work required a thick fire the fireman didn't get much rest – he'd be swinging that shovel almost continually. And all the time he was keeping the fire going he also had to watch the boiler and keep the cab clean – drivers could be fussy buggers!

'The fireman would also have to keep lookout on his side. On the Great Western the fireman was always on the left facing forward. Other areas did it differently, but for a right-handed fireman it made sense to stand on the left when it came to swinging the shovel.

'I was a fireman right up until 1965 and the end of steam, although of course I had plenty of driving when a driver fancied a rest or whatever. But I still maintain that firing was more interesting than driving. You could build up a nice regular flowing action and you were the man providing the power. It took a great deal of skill to do well because a lot of the time you had to adapt your firing technique to the particular driver. If he was a bit heavy-handed you'd need more fire; but too much fire with a good driver would be a disaster. Or you might get an engine from another railway company – a foreign engine as we used to say – and you might never really work out how to fire it.

'Foreign engines sometimes turned up because most depots covered work rostered to their areas – that meant you might get engines from elsewhere. We used to get Midland engines at Tyseley, and at Saltley they would get LNER engines now and then. I remember my dad got landed with a Southern engine once during the war and he hadn't a clue what to do with it. And remember – in those days you couldn't go and ask for a few lessons – there weren't any lessons to be had. Dad just got by as best he could working by trial and error and relying on the fact that some things were standard – all engines would have a regulator, of course – but you never really understood an engine unless you drove it regularly.'

After being promoted from shunting, Dick worked trip freight, which meant going a bit further afield to Bordesley, Handsworth, Stourbridge and Wolverhampton. On some days he might still spend a whole shift preparing engines: 'You'd be given

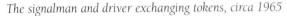

The signalman and driver exchanging tokens, circa 1965

eight engines to get ready in the time, and I can tell you it was pretty soul-destroying work,' he recalls.

Other odd days might be spent assisting a driver on the turntable or at the coal station, but eventually Dick progressed to more distant freight jobs – to Leamington, Stourbridge, Banbury, Worcester and Stratford – then local passenger trains and eventually on expresses to Bristol, Hereford, Oxford, Reading and Paddington.

'Our rosters changed every spring and summer so we might be doing any mixture of these runs and often the driver would say to me, "Come on, you drive for a bit". So I had a lot of driving experience. Some drivers never let you have a go; others would let you drive expresses. One driver I worked with for a while said he wanted to fire every other night so we took turn and turn about for a week, then on other odd occasions too.

'Driving and firing were always full of new and interesting challenges. I remember I was driver for the day with one of my regular mates and we had a brand-new engine to work to Gloucester, with a heavy freight train. Despite what you might think, a new engine is not necessarily a good thing because everything's a bit tight. I had to use more steam than you ever would normally precisely because that engine wasn't yet running as efficiently as she would when everything had loosened up a bit. Usually you'd use a lot of power to get going and then ease off. With that new engine we were never able to ease off. It was hard work all the way, but I was glad I drove it because it added to my knowledge and experience.

'Another difficulty with steam engines was that they often had to pull freight

wagons where the overall weight of the train was only vaguely calculated. All you really knew was that such and such a train would have so many wagons – you needed to know that so you could get the whole train into a loop or sidings – but for the contents of the wagons it might just say "Perishables". Well, some perishables are quite light; others, like soap for example, are as heavy as coal.'

Shunting diesels came to Tyseley in 1955, but Dick had nothing to do with them at that period. He confesses that he still feels a little sad that, after fifteen years of cleaning and firing, he didn't get the chance to spend longer driving steam, but what he had he enjoyed enormously.

'I was passed for driving in 1960, a little more than ten years after I started on the railways, but didn't became a full-time driver until 1965 just as steam disappeared. I did a lot of steam driving, as a passed fireman, but I also drove diesels for a long time – till I retired in 1993, in fact – and I can tell you that there is absolutely no comparison between driving steam and driving diesel.

'The new diesel engines were so complicated and everything – moving, starting, braking – was different. Diesels were unreliable too, in a way. If you pressed the wrong button the engine might come to a complete halt and you'd be stuck for hours in the middle of nowhere just because you didn't know where the re-set button was. With steam you could coax the engine, or do a quick repair job, so in a way diesels were more of a worry. Steam never flaked out suddenly, but diesels did.

'During the early 1960s I might be driving a steam engine one day and diesel the next – it just depended what was on the charge sheet. It was a strange time of transition, but it had its funny side, too – I remember a few drivers who didn't fancy diesels at all tried to get out of it by saying they were too dirty from years of driving steam engines and they didn't want to mess up the nice clean diesel cabs!

'We used to say that there were some jobs we'd come to work to do even if they didn't pay us – but driving diesels wasn't one of them!'

AT THE HEART OF THE GREAT WESTERN

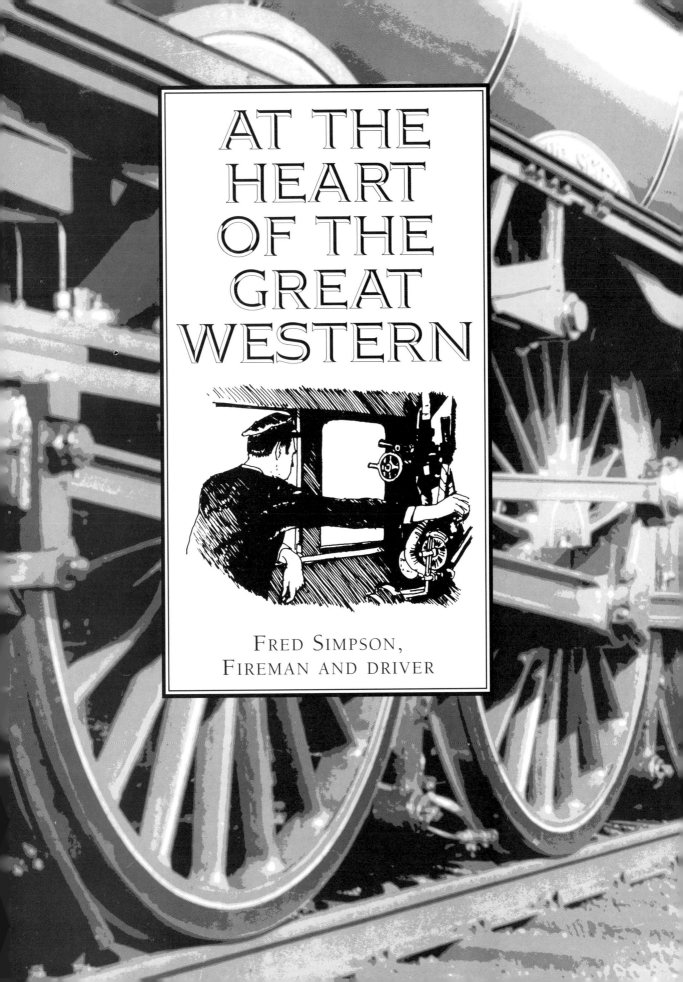

FRED SIMPSON,
FIREMAN AND DRIVER

There are probably more retired railway-men living in Swindon than in any other town in England. When you walk about the streets it's almost possible to pick them out, particularly the old footplate men who have a wiry, determined look about them. The rich architectural evidence of the railways is still there too. The great sheds, where every last nut and bolt needed by the Great Western Railway were once produced, are now converted into shopping centres, but enough remains of their solid brickwork, Victorian arches and clock towers to remind the visitor that this was once a very great railway town indeed.

Several of Swindon's old railwaymen can be seen twice a month at the local railway museum. Here they patiently explain to visitors how they once drove the huge steam engines that now stand spotless and silently gleaming around them. For these men are part of a slowly dwindling group whose like will never be seen again. They remember life on the steam railways day in, day out.

One man who knows more than most about the Great Western Railway is Fred Simpson. He was born in Swindon in 1920 and has lived there all his life. Even in old age he's tough and sinewy: his years spent on the shovel have produced the physique that somehow seems unique to railwaymen.

Fred's father had spent the whole of his working life as a machinist in the GWR factory at Swindon, and Fred joined him there as soon as he left school.

'Well, it was only natural to go into the same factory as dad. I started as an office boy and then began an apprenticeship as a brass moulder. The brass was used for all sorts of things, from boiler parts to coach doors. Everything made in that factory was used by the Great Western: they bought almost nothing in.'

In the early 1930s men counted themselves lucky to have any job at all, but an apprenticeship with the Great Western was something special. It lasted five years and covered such a wide range of skills that former railway apprentices could work virtually anywhere, as Fred explains.

'No other apprenticeship offered such thorough experience. You learned everything and, best of all, whatever the problem you learned to improvise.'

But though the job was secure it didn't suit Fred: he felt shut in. 'When I said I wanted to leave, the foreman begged me to change my mind so I think I must have been quite good!' Fred smiles and explains that it was highly unusual for an apprentice with such good prospects to leave early.

'I'd done one year out of the five by the time I packed it in, and I'm sure the foreman thought I was mad, but I went straight on to a footplate job. The factory

would have been a job for life, but the footplate was just as secure and I knew that I'd be able to retire at sixty instead of sixty-five.'

Footplate jobs were difficult to get, but Fred was already a railway employee with a good record. What's more, his mother had the bright idea of writing a letter to the foreman of the running shed, and that did the trick.

'I was in, but it was a bit of a shock – cleaning engines is the filthiest job. But several of us started on the very same day all those years ago – it was 1937 – and we're still friends now.

'Two cleaners worked one side of the engine, and two the other. You started at the front and worked towards the back; then oil up and wipe off. Easy – only most of the dirt seemed to get transferred from the engine to you! When I wasn't cleaning engines I was cycling round Swindon in the early hours of the morning knocking the drivers up. I'd knock and knock till I heard the cry – and it always seemed to be the same – "Right you be!"'

Fred explains how brick dust was rubbed on to the brasswork to make it shine, but that what really worked best was elbow grease – sheer hard work. The amount of effort that went into cleaning a particular engine could vary. 'Well, whenever we had an engine going up to Leicester we used to make sure it was absolutely perfect because at 206 miles that was a prestige job.'

The prestige aspect of the run came not just from the fact that it was a long journey, but also because it meant a Great Western engine going into the North Eastern Region. If men from elsewhere on the system were going to see that engine it had to demonstrate just what the men of the Great Western could do. Ironically, that particular engine always worked at night, so there was no one around to see how spick and span it looked. But Fred points out that after nine months in service it had been so well cared for it looked just as good as when it first came out of the shed.

After two years and six months Fred was a fireman. He's still proud of the fact that during his time as a cleaner not once did the foreman ask his cleaning gang to re-do their work.

Small boy having his ticket clipped, circa 1951
Credit: National Railway Museum/Science & Society

When a cleaner was passed for firing duties on the Great Western he was sent for a medical and then had to wait for a vacancy. When a vacancy came up you had to go, wherever it was in the region – and the Great Western covered a huge area.

'I was lucky because the war came and suddenly there were vacancies in my home town, so I stopped in Swindon. But for the war I would almost certainly have been sent to South Wales, or even Cornwall.'

Swindon was the main depot of the Great Western, although there were also depots at Bristol, Chippenham and at Old Oak Common in West London.

'Old Oak Common was the biggest depot,' explains Fred, 'and then came Bristol, and then Swindon. Surprisingly we didn't suffer that much from German bombs. All I can remember was a big one coming down in Ferndale Road, just down the way from where I live. It was close to Running Shed 1 where we were all hanging around waiting to start work. We were under a table in what we called the cabin when the bomb hit, and I can remember the ground shaking. When we came out we noticed that the huge beams that held up the roof had shifted about half an inch. They'd lifted when the bomb exploded and then resettled. Apart from that there was no damage.

'The only other incident I can recall was one day when I was out chatting to my neighbour at the end of the front garden. A German plane came in low towards us and strafed us with its machine gun – luckily it missed, but I picked up one of the bullets and I still have it!'

It was in the cabin that most of the men met at odd times between shifts. Here, around a red-hot stove, they sat on bare wooden benches and ate their sandwiches from their tin boxes.

'You couldn't buy food or a drink – no one had heard of staff canteens for railwaymen in those days, but we all had a box for our food, our tools, and of course our copies of the rule book. I always carried a spare water-gauge glass in my box. It was one of the few things that might break when you were working. It was also useful for stirring my tea!'

If the gauge broke while the engine was on the road Fred would change it, or judge his water using two test cocks – if steam and water came out of the cocks he knew he was OK. If there was no water, only steam, he knew his water was low.

When he started firing Fred worked mostly on the shunting engines, moving wagons between trains. These would usually have a driver, a fireman and a shunter.

'While I was firing the driver would look out one side of the engine, while the fireman looked out the other when not firing. We were in a very busy area so you needed all those eyes. It was actually much easier on the main line, although for the fireman it meant a lot more shovelling. You needed much more coal and water because you needed a lot more steam. When there was less time and fewer men to maintain the engines during the war, firing became much harder – a well-maintained engine is always easier because you lose less power. With a badly maintained engine you have to make up for the deficiencies.'

Among Fred's dominant memories of the war are hours spent waiting on the track in sidings and loops miles from anywhere. With bombs and disruption the days of running to time were definitely, if temporarily, over.

'I remember being in a loop at Knighton Crossing once. Six trains were held there. Eventually we had to leave the train and go home, and we came back twelve hours later to take over the same train! It often took as much as twenty-three hours to get from Swindon to Reading during the war. We'd sit there in the dark on the footplate for hours with nothing to do and – worse – nothing to eat or drink. Then when we had to work back it would take three-quarters of an hour!'

If they were stopped at a country signal miles from anywhere the footplate men would curse their luck, but sometimes things were not quite as bad.

'We used to get stopped for ages every now and then at a signal near where an aunt of mine lived. More than once we dashed off to her house for a fry-up. And at another signal there was a pub nearby – I think the men used to pray that if they were going to be held up it would be at that signal! Mind you, I did hear that, what with the war being on, as often as not they got to the pub only to find they'd run out of beer!'

Fred spent his first three years as a passed fireman firing on pannier tanks. 'They were really good little side-tank engines,' he recalls – but the lack of maintenance made even these little workhorses difficult. They were used for shunting and for local passenger work, and one or two survived the wholesale destruction of steam engines in the 1960s. For many years, as Fred explains, one helped keep London Underground going. 'For decades they kept it for shunting when the electricity failed, but I suspect it's long gone now.'

The pannier tanks might have been reliable, but like all the other engines they were badly maintained during the war. 'You wouldn't believe how the clinker used to build up in their fireboxes,' says Fred, 'and that meant too little air getting through to burn the coal properly and we lost power. On some jobs you'd arrive to find the clinker literally hanging out of the door. We had a bar to break it up, but it was a relief when we got the engine back in the shed and there was a fire dropper to do a more thorough job – fire dropping, by the way, was the worst, the dirtiest job on the railways.'

Firemen were given a test before they could take charge of a locomotive. If they failed the test three times, they could find that the only jobs still open to them were fire dropping or boiler washing or fire raising.

'Quite a number of men, for one reason or another, found themselves doing these terrible jobs permanently, but of course jobs were hard to come by and they were often grateful for whatever they could get.'

At one time there were 400 sets of footplate men at Swindon. The more experience you gained, the higher up the link you moved, but it was very much a case of moving into dead men's shoes.

'Well, dead men or retired men, anyway. Even in the links you moved up gradually until you died or retired and then that created a vacancy at the bottom. The system was that as a fireman you moved up through the pilot link, then the local passenger link, then goods, then finally passenger. Then when you were an appointed driver you started right back down at the bottom again!'

Fred fired for fifteen years – he calls it his apprenticeship – but of course throughout that time he was also driving. He's wonderfully detailed when it comes to explaining a typical day in a fireman's life.

'You got there when your shift started and signed on. That was always first. Then you'd read any notices – about speed restrictions in different places, or whatever – and you'd sign to say you'd read them. Then you studied the duty sheet to find your engine. You then looked to see where it was stabled. Next you climbed up on the footplate and immediately checked that you had enough steam and water in the boiler. The fire raisers – the men who started the fires – would usually make sure you had about 20lb pressure. You then spread the fire around and added to it. I used to make a quick check that I had all my tools: two shovels, a coal pick, fire irons and prickers to push the fire about. I'd also make sure I had my flags and detonators just in case we broke down or had to stop for some reason. I'd always have a spare gauge glass and a water-gauge spanner to shift the nuts on the gauge if I had a blow-out. This happened occasionally and was caused by a weakness in the glass. Although it often went with a bit of a bang there was a casing round it to protect your eyes.

'While the fireman made his checks the driver would check that he had what we called engine oil for the rods and what we called black oil for the lubricator, valves and pistons. We had ten minutes for booking on and fifty minutes to prepare the engine. The fireman would trim the coal in the tender and build up the fire and then we'd be ready for the off.'

Fred would sign on at 7.30 for the 9am train to London. He'd have a ton of coal in the firebox by the time he left Swindon station, and would expect to burn a further $3\frac{1}{2}$ tons to get to London and back. That's $4\frac{1}{2}$ tons of coal a day six days a week on that run, but that amount of coal – all shovelled by one man – was modest compared to the tonnage shifted by the London-to-Plymouth firemen. According to Fred's reckoning the London–Plymouth run – a distance of 226 miles – would mean the fireman had to shift more than 5 tons of coal. A lot of men joined the railway to avoid being called up during the war, but when they started firing they quickly decided the

life wasn't for them – the work was simply too hard.

On a typical shift Fred might fire from Swindon to London and back. He would have relief by another crew to take a train to Weston-Super-Mare and back, before finishing shift at 11pm. When the engine that had done the Weston-Super-Mare run was back in the shed – say at 11.15pm – it had to be left to cool, the fire cleared and made ready again to start work at 9am the next day. Then every ten days the engine would be boiler-washed.

'It had to be done every ten days,' explains Fred, 'because Swindon is a hard-water area and the limescale built up very quickly. Too much limescale would reduce efficiency. The boiler washers would also take out the plugs and the mudhole doors. They'd then put a hosepipe in and wash the whole thing clean. We had gangs of boiler washers – two in a gang – who did nothing else.'

As a passed fireman Fred did six years in No. 1 link. Then in 1955 he was appointed as a driver.

'It takes about a year now to be fully qualified as a driver,' Fred says with a rueful smile. 'In my day twenty years was common, but it was important because it's experience that runs a railway. In an emergency it's the man with experience who will usually know what to do.'

But even though he was a fully registered driver Fred had to go right back down to the bottom link. 'Although I was fully qualified I found myself back on the pilots. I didn't mind. No one did in those days. It wasn't like a demotion or anything – it was just the way things were done and it was the same for everyone.'

Drivers and firemen almost invariably enjoyed good relations, Fred recalls, and even a fully made-up driver would still give his fireman a hand now and then.

'Of course you might swap for a bit just to keep your hand in – that way the fireman got a bit more driving practice – but for most of the time driving meant keeping an eye on the road and on your fireman. The great thing you have to remember about driving a steam engine is that it only got where it was going because of you and your fireman.'

Driver and fireman on the footplate of a 4-6-0 Schools Class steam locomotive, circa 1957
Credit: National Railway Museum/Science & Society

Fred's experience in the factory as a lad just out of school stood him in good stead throughout his driving career because he believes that a locomotive is a workshop on wheels. But the nature of these workshops varied enormously. Fred worked on Castles with their big, relatively comfortable cabs, but at the other extreme he also remembers the little standard goods engines with no cab at all.

But what about driving itself? It seemed easy to Fred, but then he was enormously experienced by the time he first took control.

'On paper it does sound easy,' he says with a grin. 'You just made sure you had enough pressure and opened the regulator. As soon as you did that you'd start moving. As you picked up a bit of speed you'd notch her up a bit to conserve steam. This just meant operating a lever to shorten the travel of the valves – sounds complicated, but it was really just like changing gear on a car. Shortening the travel of the valves meant you were making the steam do the work and burning less coal. You'd go for a 25 per cent cut-off on the valves at 45mph; for more power you might drop the lever to 35 per cent.'

People who have only travelled by diesel and electric train often forget how powerful some of the old steam engines really were. The Castles would comfortably run at 70 or 80mph, occasionally touching 90mph. 'In certain places and with a reasonable load we often did that,' says Fred.

Braking was also achieved using steam, and again the system was remarkably reliable – unless the rubber sealing rings in the cylinders failed. 'If that happened you

Fred (seated right) with a group of retired GWR drivers at Steam, the railway museum in Swindon

would have no brakes,' says Fred. 'But remember, those rings would have to fail on all the pistons for you to have really serious problems.'

There were many challenges for the steam engine driver as he coaxed his engine along the road, not least of which was the huge difference between passenger and goods trains.

'On the passenger link you had solid couplings,' explains Fred, 'and on goods trains they were loose couples. When you were pulling you had to contend with gaps between the wagons. This meant that when you were braking with a goods train you had to ease the brake on gently, or all the wagons would end up in a heap behind you. Braking gently would buffer up the wagons before you applied the full brake. The truth is that any idiot can be taught to drive – braking is the tricky bit. And you had to do it in plenty of time. On a passenger link we'd normally start braking about a mile before the station. and it was rare not to stop right on the button.'

Punctuality was also important, and Fred laughs when he remembers one foggy day when a passenger at Reading ran up to the cab and told him that he had to catch a plane, and needed to be at Paddington on time.

'He thought it was down to us, as if we were driving a car. The truth is that the whole system was geared up to keeping trains on time. Mind you, when we got to Paddington he ran back up to the cab and gave me half a crown, so he obviously thought we'd made a special effort!'

When diesel finally came in Fred recalls that at first the drivers thought it was fine, but soon found it boring.

'With steam you had to use your loaf. You had to work with your fireman to make a success of it and it could be hard – sometimes you had to nurse the thing along. With diesel the engine told you what was wrong; with steam only experience would tell you when there was a problem and how best to deal with it.

'But to go back to my firing days – they were hard, much harder than driving. I can remember once late at night coming back towards Swindon from London and I thought my arms were going to drop off! Oddly, too, it made a lot of difference if you had a good shovel, which is why you hung on to it when you got one.'

Fred drove diesels from 1967 until 1977 when he retired. He'd had enough of shifts that began at 2am, and without steam engines a lot of the magic had gone. Gone too now are all the running sheds at Swindon.

'I worked one of the very last steam trains – from Andover at 12.30pm one Sunday. The people of Andover came out to wave us off and it was a very sad day indeed.

'I don't miss the railway now, but I miss the steam engines and the men I worked with. I enjoyed it all, which is why I still go twice a month to the museum to explain to visitors what it was once like.'

Finishing touches being applied to steam locomotive No 70000 Britannia *in the paintshop at Crewe Works, 1951
Credit: National Railway Museum/Science & Society*

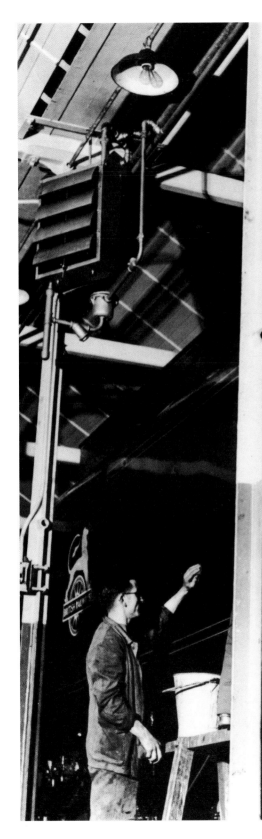